# So, Its Laughs You Want!

## Jokes – Gags - snickers & Bits of Business for the stage show entertainer

A strange collection of humor, satire, bits of business and garbage exclusively for the stage show entertainer.

**Compiled by L. Wade Johnson**

**So, It's Laughs You Want**

**So, its Laughs You Want**

***I dedicate this book to me for without me this book would have never been written.***

So, its laughs you want is the result of 63 years of wasted time.

This is no ordinary joke book, it was written for the performer who wants laughs. If its Laughs you want you got them here, sure fire tested, wholesome comedy material.

Included in this material are set up lines, comedy activities, one liners and general funny stuff organized by topic.

Printed in Inglesh

ISBN-13:
978-1545458662

ISBN-10:
1545458669

**Acknowledgements**

I am indebted to Sheila Butler who took many of my handwritten notes and converted them to a useable digital format for publishing.

After 92 pages, we decided to call it quits and save the rest for another book.

To my wife, Sharon Amore Thomas Johnson who has put up with my jokes and overall silliness for the past fifty plus years. There must be a special place in God's kingdom for wives like her.

**1705010909**

## Table of Contents

**Good Luck with this!**

## Air Conditioning

We have an unusual breakdown in the air conditioning system. The truck broke down so our air conditioner hasn't been delivered yet. That was in 2007,

I think that office group is a bunch of home sick Eskimos. They can't work unless their teeth are chattering.

He drives an air-conditioned car from his air-conditioned office to his air-conditioned club, so he can take a steam bath,

It's cold in here. The management has the air conditioner turned up to Siberia again.

They said this place was air conditioned, and I have never seen air in such a condition.

What to do about all the wealth in the hands of air condition repairmen!

## Ambiguities

1. Don't sweat the petty things and don't pet the sweaty things.

2. One tequila, two tequila, three tequila, floor....

3. Atheism is a non-prophet organization.

5. The main reason Santa is such a jolly being because he knows where all the naughty girls live.

6. I went to a bookstore and asked the saleswoman, "Where's the self-help section?"
She said if she told me, it would defeat the purpose.

8. If a deaf person swears, does his mother wash his hands with soap?

## Aphorisms

It's not whether you win or lose, but how you place the blame.

We have enough "youth". How about a fountain of "smart"?

A Fool and his money can throw one heck of a party.

When blondes have more fun, do they know it?

We are born naked, wet and hungry. Then things get worse.

Ninety-nine percent of all lawyers give the rest a bad name.

ARTIFICIAL INTELLIGENCE IS NO MATCH FOR NATURAL STUPIDITY.

The latest survey shows that three out of four people make up 75% of the population.

"I think Congressmen should wear uniforms, you know, like NASCAR drivers, so we could identify their corporate sponsors..."

The reason Politicians try so hard to get re-elected is that they would 'hate' to have to make a living under the laws they've passed.

## Armed Forces

And the mess sergeant was always complaining. He said, "Eight hours I spend behind the stove, and all I get is complaints." he's lucky, I got indigestion.

But every time I went on guard duty I took an oath. I said if anything moves I'll shoot, and if anything shoots I'll move!

Every morning we had to take our rifles apart. And in ten minutes I had mine all together again, in a neat little pile.

Speaking of guns, I'll never forget the time we went to the rifle range. We knelt at 300 yards and fired no hits. Then again at 200 yards, again no hits. Then at 100 yards and still no one hit the target. The sergeant turned and yelled, "Fix bayonets and charge. It's your only chance,"

But all in all, army life wasn't so bad. Take army food. I wish somebody would.

The way to tell a sailor from a marine? When a girl passes and the man whistles, it's a sailor. If the girl whistles, it's a marine.

He tried on his old Army uniform and all that fits is the tie.

Sometimes I wonder about West Point. Are they trying to build an Army to beat Russia or Navy?

When I was in the Navy, I was always A.W.O.L. (After Women or Liquor)

SARGEANT: You're out of uniform. PFC: No, but I'd like to be.

SARGEANT: Don't these stripes mean anything to you?
PFC: No, a zebra is covered with them and underneath, he's still a jack ass.

What a Drill Instructor! His voice has stripes in it.

I got a GI haircut in boot camp and it hasn't healed yet.

I was a second Lieutenant. I was too young to be a private.

## Band lines

***Gags to use when working with a band***

They would have liked to have had a hit record on that song. But they didn't.

They did record that song, but they had already the CD in the stores when they realized the CD was blank. And it became a hit!

You call that a lead in? It sounds more like an all clear signal for a floating crap game.

This is our band, Danny, and the Dressmakers

This is our band Curt Carlson and the Carrol County car strippers.

They are called by many names. None of which we can use here.

(Lift the drummer's cymbal). What! Pot roast again?

Fellas, could you hold it down a little bit, it's too loud. A little bit more, more. I can still hear you.

They are accomplished musicians in their own right. I don't know what they are going for these days but I saw their pictures hanging in the post office and the Government is offering thousand dollars apiece for them.

They have had a lot of requests for this next song. But they are gonna do it anyway.

They don't usually do requests, unless they are asked.

Thank you for that wonderful rendition of. . . well I don't know what that was.

We believe there is nothing like good music, and believe me that was nothing like good music.

They do country music, and blue grass. Well not really blue grass, it is more like crab grass.

Yeah, we're paying this band by the hour

One: Speaking of the band, let me introduce you to these guys, that is (Name of banjo player) on the plinkity plink banjo

Two: Make that a blankety blank banjo and I'll agree with you,

**So, It's Laughs You Want**

One: (name of guitar player), on guitar, he plays the hottest guitar in town

Two: Yeah, he stole it two hours ago.

We just completed a tour of the Southern States with world famous band. The Salvation Army band.

Ventriloquist: This next song is one of your favorites.

Dummy: It aint one of mine I'll tell you right now.

Dummy: Hey band leader. You got any idea why we don't have any hit records?
Band Leader: You got me.
Dummy: That's the reason.

(When working with an orchestra or a band with music sheets). If you want to know what that paper is in front of them. That's the score. I think the drummer is winning.

Some drummer. Sounds like a beer truck running over a man hole cover.

(Band plays introduction song) Would you play that again please?
(Band plays it the same way) Oh excuse me I thought you played it wrong there. (to audience) well folks, you can't blame me. They're cheap.

Is that a new drummer, or did the old one take a bath?

Take a look at that band. Looks like a police lineup on a Monday morning.

Wow! You guys have never played better. Kinda sad when you think about it.

## Bits of Business

Isn't that exciting? I'll get a party hat.

(New York Skyline). Want to buy a dirty picture.

Supermarket? Should be super mark-up.

49c for a handy bottle or $2,000 for a truck load.

They stand behind every bed they sell. I hope they don't peek.

I bought a collapsible swimming pool. This morning it collapsed.

Lone applauder: I thought I told you to wait in the truck.

Lone applauder: I'll tell you what, you watch everybody else, and when they applaud, you join in.

Lone applauder: Thanks, a lot Mom

Lone applauder: I'll tell you what. Why don't you stand up? Maybe someone will recognize you and take you home.

Lone applauder: Excuse me Ahh, (sir or mam) what show are you watching?

Lone applauder: What are you doing? Trying to keep yourself awake?

Someone walking out: Hey buddy, get back in here. You're no better than the rest of them.

Someone walking out: Hey, where ya going? Coffee, you'll get sick!

Someone walking out: Ah huh, I know where you were. And you were writing on the walls again

Someone walking out: What is this? I-95?

Well-shaped girl walks by: Lookie, lookie, what a cookie!

Well-shaped girl walks by: That reminds me, I have to have my watch fixed.

Well-shaped girl walks by: Oh, if my watch only had a movement like that.

Dropped speech: I've heard of a speech falling flat, but this is ridiculous!

Dropped Speech: You can't blame me for being nervous. I live in a high-risk neighborhood---Earth!

Rebuttal: I couldn't swallow that if it came with an olive!

After dead microphone repaired: I'm glad you fixed that! For a while there I was beginning to feel like I was doing a pantomime!

Small audience: I haven't seen anything this empty since I looked in the suggestion box at the Kremlin.

Someone laughing louder than the others: I like you! You are a good audience all by yourself.

## Blonde Jokes

A married couple were asleep when the phone rang at 2 in the morning. The very blonde wife picked up the phone, listened a moment and said; 'How should I know; that's 200 miles from here!' and hung up. The husband said, 'Who was that?'
The wife answered, 'I don't know, some woman wanting to know if the coast is clear.'

Two blondes are walking down the street. One notices a compact on the sidewalk and leans down to pick it up. She opens it, looks in the mirror and says, 'Hmm, this person looks familiar.' The second blonde says, 'Here, let me see!' So, the first blonde hands her the compact. The second blonde looks in the mirror and says, 'You dummy, it's me!'

A blonde suspects her boyfriend of cheating on her, so she goes out and buys a gun. She goes to his apartment unexpectedly and when she opens the door she finds him in the arms of a redhead. Well, the blonde is really angry. She opens her purse to take out the gun, and as she does so, she is overcome with grief. She takes the gun and puts it to her head. The boyfriend yells, 'No, honey, don't do it!!!' The blonde replies, 'Shut up, you're next!'

A blonde was bragging about her knowledge of state capitals. She proudly says, 'Go ahead, ask me, ... I know 'em all.' A friend says, 'OK, what's the capital of Wisconsin?' The blonde replies, 'Oh, that's easy . it's W.'

Q: What did the blonde ask her doctor when he told her she was pregnant?
A: 'Is it mine?'

Bambi, a blonde in her fourth year as a UCLA Freshman, sat in her U.S. Government class. The professor asked Bambi if she knew what Roe vs. Wade was about. Bambi pondered the question; then, finally, said, 'That was the decision George Washington had to make before he crossed the Delaware.'

Returning home from work, a blonde was shocked to find her house ransacked and burglarized. She telephoned the police at once and reported the crime. The police dispatcher broadcast the call on the radio, and a K-9 unit, patrolling nearby, was the first to respond. As the K-9 officer approached the house with his dog on a leash, the blonde ran out on the porch, shuddered at the sight of the cop and his dog, then sat down on the steps. Putting her face in her hands, she moaned, 'I come home to find all my possessions stolen. I call the police for help, and what do they do? They send me a BLIND policeman!'

The radio announcer said the snow plows would plow the odd side of the street tomorrow so everyone must move their car to the even side of the road. Mrs. Hatfield moved her car as instructed. That night, the announcer informed the citizens they had to move their cars to the odd side of the road so the plows could plow the odd side. Mrs. Hatfield was irritated by the event but she dutifully moved her car. The snow continued and each night the citizens were told to move their cars. When it was announced again on the fourth day she exclaimed to her husband; "I am getting tired of moving my car each night." Her husband replied, well, dear why don't you just leave it in the garage tonight?

## Cars & Driving

The nimblest person in the world is the man who can change gears in a smart without getting his face slapped!

A group of boys were tearing down the road in a 1995 Ford. One boy, seeing that his door wasn't closed, opened it, and slammed it shut, the driver looked back and said, "Hey who just got in?"

An old woman was driving a big car and she ran over a man. She got out and said; "Young man you better watch out!" He looked up and said weakly, "My gosh lady! Don't tell me you're going to back up!"

This is the Holiday weekend; the National Safety Council says they're going to be 420 persons killed on highways in traffic accidents. So far there are only 120 killed. Some of you folks aren't trying."

We must be getting closer to town, we're hitting more people!

I just put a new gadget in my car to keep the inside quiet. It fits over her mouth!

With twenty million autos in the world today, this is going to be a heck of a place for a horse fly.

**So, It's Laughs You Want**

I just bought a new car! It has so much power it could climb any hill you put in front of it! But it got over anxious and tried to climb up a telephone pole.

What traffic! I drove three miles before I realize my motor had been stolen!

Two hoodlums were caught stealing cars. The police put them up against the squad car and began frisking them. One hood turned and said; "Hey man, you won't find any cars in there!"

A passenger in a taxi leaned over to ask the driver a question and tapped him on the shoulder. The driver screamed, lost control of the cab, nearly hit a bus, drove up over the curb, and stopped just inches from a large plate glass window. For a few moment's everything was silent in the cab, and then the still shaking driver said, 'I'm sorry, but you scared the Hell out of me!' The frightened passenger apologized to the driver and said he didn't realize a mere tap on the shoulder could frighten him so much. The driver replied, 'No, no, I'm sorry, it's entirely my fault. Today is my first day driving a cab.... I've been driving a hearse for the last 25 years.'

Henry Ford, all those millions and he never owned a Cadillac.

My car is so small I have to pay my traffic tickets in Juvenile Court.

I won't say California drivers are wild, but if you drive under fifty, you're double parked.

Talk about bad luck...I bought a set of snow tires, and they melted.

Professor goes camping in a book mobile.

I don't mind them sending a woman astronaut to the moon as long as the get someone else to do the parking.

He has antique cars. He says its antique. To him, an antique car is a Cadillac no longer under warranty.

What a great car! The windshield wipers won't hold a parking ticket.

Japanese cars have 4 speeds. 1st, 2nd, 3rd, and Bonsai

I call my car flattery, because it gets me nowhere.

If all cars in America were lined up end to end, it would be like . . . Labor Day.

Those foreign cars that have been imported have certainly solve the traffic problem. Solved it in Japan, France, and England.

That car is so big, it takes 6 minutes to go through a one minute car wash.

Since I bought that car, there has been one happy man in this town. The salesman.

That's the only car I've ever seen that was held together by a paint job.

My wife drives like she's rehearsing for an accident.

She finally got the hang of driving after a while, though, now at least the road turns when she does.

Some people just don't know how to drive...I call these people "Everybody but Me."

Don't like my driving? Then quit watching me.

Oh, she is a great driver. When she drives through town other motorists drive up on the sidewalk to watch her. Cops take notes!
Ever notice that anyone going slower than you is an idiot, but anyone going faster is a maniac?

Car sickness is the feeling you get when the monthly payment is due.

## Bumper Stickers

My Father does not approve of this.

Don't laugh its paid for.

I drive too fast to worry about cholesterol.

If you can read this...I can slam on my brakes and sue you.

I'm retired. Go around me!

## Cheap Skates

Boy, is he cheap! When he picks up his own check, he's treating!

I won't say he's cheap, but if two guys are having lunch and one reached for the check, he would be the other guy!

He talks through his nose to keep from wearing out his teeth.

He orders two graham crackers and a glass of milk. Three, if he's hungry!

He's so cheap, on the Fourth of July all he does is snap his fingers!

You know what I like about him? Nothing!

Cheap! She bought a ten gallon can of hair spray, pressed the button and blew her arm off!

Cheap! He takes off his glasses when he's not looking at anything!

## Children

I just read about another set of twins being born. I think kids are afraid to come into this world alone.

My mother loved children.... too bad she never had any.

I used to hang out with a tough gang, when I was fiver years old I was head repaint man for a hot tricycle ring.

I wanted to be like other ten-year-old boys, go out on hikes, play ball, neck with girls, steal cars, slug cops.

I used to sing in a choir, but my voice was so high I had to sing with the girls. When I got old enough to enjoy it, my voice changed.

Little boys should be seen, not hurt.

Ventriloquist: I was cute when I was delivered by the stork.
Dummy: You weren't delivered by a stork, you were delivered by a buzzard.

Do you know how much a baby costs? Over five thousand dollars! Yeah, but look how long they last!

I was born in Boston. We didn't have any real bird life in Boston. The stork had to deliver me to Providence, then American Express took me the rest of the way!

At the age of three, I was left an orphan. Now at three years old, what would I do with an orphan?

I was born December 24th. I wanted to be home for Christmas!

When I was born, the doctor rushed in and shouted "Congratulations!! I think it's a baby!"

I came from a tough neighborhood. If you had your teeth, you were a sissy!

I remember when kids used to run away from home. Now they defect!

Dirty! After my kid takes a bath I have to dredge the tub!

My kid came back from camp yesterday. He brought back a hand-carved ashtray. I treasure that ash tray. The way I figure it, that ashtray cost me $800!

When I first picked up the baby, my wife said, "Watch the baby's head" But it wasn't the head I had to watch!

One: We have a new bouncing baby.

Two: Boy or girl?

Two: I don't know, hasn't stopped bouncing yet.

We feed the baby garlic, so we can find it in the dark!

When I was a kid, I was a track star in school. I sold racing forms.

Oh, to be a baby again. To sit on a woman's lap without buying her a mink coat!

I read about a woman who had triplets. Science says that triplets happen only once in 200,000 times. I wonder how she found time to do her housework.

The first time I walked I took 23 steps. I fell down the front stairs.

My neighborhood was so poor, if you paid you rent 2 months in advance, the police wanted to know where you got the money.

When I was 12 years old, my father told me not to go to burlesque shows, or I would see something I wasn't supposed to see. So, the first chance I got, I went to one, and I did see something I wasn't supposed to see...my father!

The only cure for kids like him is birth control!

"Who shot Abe Lincoln?"
"I don't squeal on nobody!"

When he was 8 years old, his parents ran away from home.

He received a scholarship to a reform school.

**So, It's Laughs You Want**

He was 6 foot 3. He got a haircut, now he's 5 foot 7!

Here's a great name for a birth control pill--"No kidding.":

When I was a kid, we had a swimming pool in our front yard. The city called it a clogged sewer.

My kids had trouble packing for camp this year--the TV wouldn't fit in the suitcase with the stereo.

I just took on four new dependents — (Name three prominent investment firms).

I was tough when I was a kid. When we played Hop Scotch, we used real Scotch!

Kids in the back-seat cause accidents. Accidents in the back-seat cause kids.

I want my children to have all the things I couldn't afford. Then I want to move in with them.

Most children threaten at times to run away from home. This is the only thing that keeps some parents going.

We spend the first twelve months of our children's lives teaching them to walk and talk and the next twelve telling them to sit down and shut up.

Tranquilizers work only if you follow the advice on the bottle - keep away from children.

The best way to keep kids at home is to make a pleasant atmosphere - and let the air out of their tires.

## Christmas

Frosty the snowman gets hot and bothered. By the time, he decides to cool it, He's just a big drip.

If you have ever seen those post office lines, you would understand why Santa Claus delivers his own presents.

Santa Claus is my kind of guy. He only works one day a year.

I gave her something for her head. Hair

Rudolph the red nosed reindeer looked out the window and said to his wife, "It's raining." His wife said, "No, sweetheart, it's snowing." With which Rudolf replied, "Rudolph the red knows rain, dear."

Here it is two weeks after Christmas and we're still cleaning. Last week we cleaned out our checking account, and this week we cleaned out the savings account.

Santa Claus is not a myth, heth a mithter.

If you're looking for a gift for me, my hand first a Cadillac steering wheel.

I don't want much for Christmas, just a 5-pound box of money.

Yeah, he took off his stock and stood them by the fireplace.

She said, "put the turkey in the oven and turn for 3 hours." After the first hour, I was so dizzy I could hardly stand up.

I don't care who you are, fatso, get your reindeer off my roof.

This year my wife want to give sensible gifts like ties and mink coats.

I didn't join the Christmas club because I knew I couldn't attend the meetings.

Do your Christmas shop lifting early.

Santa Claus saw him and stopped believing in people.

Not all Christmas cards come in the mail. Some show up at Christmas parties.

He won a turkey at a raffle . . . he held.

Tonight, we slither through the silly selections Santa Style

Santa's holiday hits for happy hippies, a cool collection.

**So, It's Laughs You Want**

Of kooky cards for krazy kids and goofy grown up,

Vocalized by the Varicose Voices of (Ventriloquial team)

What I don't like about office Christmas parties is looking for a job the next day.

## Cities, States, and other Places

Suburbia: where they tear out the trees & then name streets after them.

I just got home from Hollywood. Boy, what a walk, (Las Vegas)

You can't exactly call Las Vegas a city. It's more like a garbage disposal for money.

The last time I went to Las Vegas, I lost 42 dollars in a gum machine.

Las Vegas is gambling crazy. I dropped a dime in the parking meter and 3 little wheels spun around and I lost my car.

You know why Las Vega is so crowded? No one has any plane fare to leave.

I love Las Vegas. You can't beat the climate, the sun, the night life, the slot machines.

A Martian landed in Las Vegas. He spends a half hour watching people play a slot machine. Finally, he goes over to the slot machine and says, "Buddy, I don't know what office you're running for, but when you shake hands, you'd better smile."

I drove to Las Vegas in a $40,000 car and came back in a $140,000 bus!

I was thinking about taking a 9 to 5 job in Las Vegas but I didn't like the odds.

I guess you all know I was born in Paris - Paris Island.

You can tell it's a rough neighborhood. When the Salvation Army passed the hat, they didn't get it back.

One: The Southland is God's country.

Two: Of course, it's God's country. You didn't think God was a Yankee, did you?

**So, It's Laughs You Want**

The town is 45 minutes from the nearest city - by telephone.

Ahh, California, land of silken honeys.

You know why Russia is doing so good in her negotiations? It's the only country in the world that isn't afraid of communism.

Ventriloquist: The town fathers wanted to build something in our memory.

Dummy: They're going to erect an outhouse in our honor.

The mayor gave us the key to the city. Somebody locked us out.

Don't worry about the Russian's threat to bury us. With the price of American funerals, they couldn't afford it.

America! The only country where business men can sit around talking about hard times over a fifty-dollar steak.

The pollution is so thick in Chicago, you don't breathe the air, you chew it.

With all these good will tours the State Departments making, why is it that we don't have any good will?

I am no longer responsible for the debts of the U.S. Government.

We just made a reciprocal trade agreement with Russia. We agreed to send 20,000 cars from Detroit and they agreed to send 40,000 parking spaces from Siberia.

Some Texans don't believe in Heaven or Hell. They believe, that when they die, they will either go to Dallas or Alaska.

Texans have a right to be mad. So now, they are the second largest state. They can accept that. It's those care packages from Fairbanks that really hurt.

I was in Alaska last week. What a great place. I took a ride on a cross-town bus that barked.

**So, It's Laughs You Want**

Want a real thrill? I love to play golf in Alaska. You hit a ball down the fairway and by the time it stops rolling, it's four feet wide.

Traffic sign in downtown Fairbanks, Alaska - mush and Don't Mush.

Just my luck. I went to Florida when it was cold. I had to put anti-freeze in my suntan lotion.

Who says the American dollar doesn't go far? It goes to Indo China, that's pretty far.

We visited the Roman Coliseum. It looks like my Landlord is maintaining it.

I remember when Russia was known for its caviar, instead of its baloney.

I didn't realize this town was so close to ahh......Nowhere, Nowhere.

In that town, the most dangerous job is riding shotgun on a garbage truck.

I don't know why we're having so much trouble in Africa. We have the phantom, Jungle Jim, Tarzan. Some body is not trying?

His new address: 27369288 - a box car.

Texas doesn't even celebrate George Washington's birthday. They figure a guy who never told a lie isn't worth remembering.

Washington is first in war, first in peace, and last in the American League.

You see all this cold weather? I told them they would have trouble if they let Alaska in the

Union.

I was through that town last year. Got a ticket for running a Landmark. They had a stop light on a one-way street.

Nobody ever dies here. (Funeral) Undertaker starved to death.

Mind reader went to Hollywood and starved to death.

Texans don't ask you where you're from, they figure if they are from Texas you will tell them, if you are not why embarrass you?

## Closing Lines

I want to thank you from the bottom of my check book.

Ventriloquist: I want to thank you from the bottom of my heart.
Dummy: I also want to thank you from my bottom.

I have to be going now. If I'm not home by twelve o'clock, my landlady rents out the room.

I need a little help on this one. When I count to three, will everybody stomp three times? (Stomp) Thanks. I just got into an argument with the janitor downstairs and I just wanted to irritate him.

And on behalf of the management, I'd like to say that. . .I'd like to be half of the management.

And so, in closing, let me leave you with the world of a famous horticulturist, Luther Luther Burbank, who said "Never look down on a lily. Tomorrow that lily may be looking down on you!

## Clothes

That's a nice fur coat. Did you kill it yourself?

Get a load of that jacket, somewhere in New Jersey there is a '56 Chevrolet without any seat covers.

You wanna know what keeps that strapless evening gown up? I'll tell you - a city ordinance.

I like that suit. I think I know the guy who was buried in it.

She's the only woman I know who has nothing to wear and needs 2 closets to keep it in.

I usually wear a cape, but it's Superman's turn this week. (or Dracula)

See those spots on the lapel? That's rust. This suit wears like iron.

This suit will not shrink, unless it gets wet.

He has a rainbow tie. It even has a pot at the end.

That is an Italian tie. You can tell, it has a pizza stain on it.

I like this hat. I had it cleaned once, change it in a restaurant twice, and it's still good as new.

This hat cost me 185 bucks! Actually, I only paid $6 for it when I bought it, but it costs me a dollar every time I get it back from a hat check girl.

**So, It's Laughs You Want**

See this shirt? This shirt cost me 185 bucks! Actually, I only paid $6 for it when I bought it, but when cost me six bucks every time I get it back from the laundry!

The last time I lent a guy my tuxedo, I had to dig him up to get it back.

That's a reversible jacket. Turn it inside out and it's a badminton court.

It's shrink resistant. It still shrinks, but it doesn't want to.

She bought a $500 wig. I'll tell you, Jesse James never had a price like that on his head.

He puts shoe trees in his sneakers.

Just like a Chinese laundry, two hours after your clothes are cleaned, they're dirty again.

In a tux: I feel like I just fell off a wedding cake.

All dressed up, like a well-kept grave.

Is that your hat or is your head shaped that way?

The Police described her costume as next to nothing. I have news for him. That costume was next to plenty.

What a swim suit! I've seen more cotton in a bottle of aspirin.

Now there's a becoming gown. And if she doesn't watch out, it will be coming off.

That's a play suit? What kind of games do you play?

Suit holds a crease. Holds thousands of them.

One: You certainly have comfortable bedroom slippers.

Two: How do you know?

One: I have them on.

And the dress she wore kept everybody warm but her.

My friend here is very expensively garbed. And believe me, I know expensive garbage.

She claims she wears her clothes to attract men. Now that's silly! She could probably attract more men without clothes!

How do you like this coat? I picked it up in New York....When no one was looking!

This coat has a tear in it. I'll just wear it without any pants and no one will notice.

Just got my jacket back from the cleaners. It looks just as good now as it did when the Salvation Army gave it to me.

**So, It's Laughs You Want**

It looks like you really live in that coat! Looks like you take in roomers too.

Look at that hat. I've seen a better lid on a garbage can.

She dresses like a lady.... Lady Godiva.

Her neck line is where her waist line should be.

Her slacks are so tight, if she had a coin in her pocket, you could tell if it was head or tails.

That suit is very becoming......becoming extinct!

I'll bet your tailor wears sun glasses when he presses that suit!

That swimsuit is guaranteed not to shrink! How can it shrink smaller!?

That's an expensive gown. It's not the cost that bothers me, it's the up keep.

I bought a pair of shoes from a drug dealer. I don't what he laced them with but I have been tripping all day!

## College – Schools - Education

He wanted to go to college to avoid the draft, so he registered in West Point.

College is of some value. It cured my mother of bragging about me.

Notre Dame....a stadium with an adjoining college.

I remember the old water fountain at our school? Old Face full. (faithful)

I'm not going back to school until the dean takes back what he said. What did he say? He said, "Get out and stay out!"

One: I didn't go to classes today. I didn't feel well.
Two: Where didn't you feel well?
One: In class...

College full of beautiful girls. I'll have to pace myself. I hope my roommate can handle the overflow.

**So, It's Laughs You Want**

One: As soon as we arrived, we met Sgt. Johnson.

Two: Dean.

One: Dean Johnson. (Like made a mistake)

I even flunked recess.

I wrote a term paper. I made a paper airplane out of it and someone hijacked it.

Talk about loving literature our professor goes camping in bookmobile.

Everyone in my third-grade class was proud of me when I joined the Marines.

I spent my mornings in school, and afternoons in the pool room. It's a shame the way I wasted those mornings.

I was in high school so long that they didn't give me a diploma, they gave me an eviction notice.

I left college because of girl trouble. They didn't have any girls, that was the trouble.

I was the most advanced pupil in my class. All the other kids were 8...I was 22

I made all the kids in my class look sick. I had the measles and they all caught it.

I was going to drop Philosophy, but I couldn't. I needed the sleep.

They handed me the sheep skin with this little phrase. "We should have skinned you and graduated the sheep."

I miss those good ole school days. That's why the truant officer followed me around. I missed those good ole school days every chance I got.

I was a track star in college. I sold racing forms.

There wasn't a single student in Georgia Tech in the same class with me. I didn't go to Georgia Tech.

I'm finally getting out of college and not a dollar too soon.

**So, It's Laughs You Want**

I got a letter in my senior year . . . from the Dean asking me if I was going to leave.

They don't buy football players. The give them room and board and $2000 a week for books.

Books for sale...hardly used. Grades to prove it.

Teacher: Are you learning anything?

Student: No, I'm listening to you.

One: That isn't good English.

Two: Where's your grammar?

One: She's home with my Grandfather

He dropped out of kindergarten.... when he was 10

You talk about educated! He has more degrees than a thermometer

The trouble I had in school were the teachers. They kept flunking me.

One: I'm worried about increasing my IQ.
Two: Don't worry about it, it's nothing.

You talk about a tough school, we had the only school newspaper with an obituary column.

## Cops and Robbers

Two police officers responding to a domestic disturbance with shots fired arrive on scene. After discovering the wife had shot her husband for walking across her freshly mopped floor, they call their sergeant on his cell phone.

"Hello Sarge."

"Yes."

"It looks like we have a homicide here. "

"What happened?"

"A woman has shot her husband for walking on the floor
she had just mopped."

"Have you placed her under arrest?"

"No sir. The floor is still wet. "

## Courts

I don't like the jury system. How can you send six men and six women in a room overnight and come out and say; "Not guilty?"

Judge: When were you born?
Man: I don't know, Judge, I was just a little baby.

Judge: Guilty or not guilty?
Man: If I tell you now it will spoil the trial!

The defendant is out on bail and the jury is locked up for the night.

Judge: Have you been up before me?
Defendant: I don't know Judge, what time did you get up?

Didn't you see that red light?
Ah, Judge, you see one, you see 'em all!

Judge: OK, I'll give it to you short and fast. And I want the truth!
Defendant: Well, that will take a little longer.

## Crime, stealing, crooks and cheats

Crime doesn't pay, but the hours are good.

This guy is so crooked, the wool he pulls over your eyes is 50% cotton.

He counts his money in front of a mirror...he doesn't even trust himself.

I hear a burglar. Quiet, if he finds anything worth stealing, we'll jump him and take it.

He has a police record. He was on the force for three years.

If they can't control crime, why don't they legalize it and tax it out of business.

Do you like killing and robbing innocent people? No. Then why do you do it? It gives me something to do.

I don't like the word stealing. Redistributions is a much better word.

You'll think of something. Just use that slinky, conniving, devious mind of yours. Ahh, you left out sneaky.

He is so crooked, he pays his bribes in counterfeit money.

He is so crooked, he has to screw on his socks.

He's two faced, and they're both ugly.

He is not two faced. If he was he would be wearing the other one.

He keeps 3 sets of books - one of himself, one for his partner and one for the government.

One: Are you shot bad?

Two: Have you ever seen anyone who was shot good?

A burglar found an old maid under his bed.

One: Now, these are villains. They get paid plenty for being bad.

Two: I don't have to be paid for being the good guy. I'm good for nuthin'.

One: There was a robbery and I got one of them!
Two: Which one?
One: The one that was robbed!

**So, It's Laughs You Want**

He stole a TV set and would have gotten away clean, but two weeks later he was arrested. He just couldn't resist mailing in that 90-day warranty!

Any time three New Yorkers get into a cab without an argument, a bank has just been robbed.

**Daffynitions**

ADULT: A person who has stopped growing at both ends and is now growing in the middle.

BEAUTY PARLOR: A place where women curl up and dye.

BOSS: Someone who is early when you are late and late when you are early

CANTELOPE: When you can't runoff and get married.

BEGGER: One who practices beggary

CHICKENS: The only animals you eat before they are born and after they are dead.

COMMITTEE: A body that keeps minutes and wastes hours.

DUST: Mud with the juice squeezed out.

EGOTIST: Someone who is usually me-deep in conversation.

HANDKERCHIEF: Cold Storage.

INFLATION: Cutting money in half without damaging the paper.

INSOMNIA: When you can't sleep until it's time to get up.

MOSQUITO: An insect that makes you like flies better.

POLITITIAN: One who can straddle a fence and still keep both ears to the ground

RAISIN: A grape with a sunburn.

SECRET: Something you tell to one person at a time.

SKELETON: A bunch of bones with the person scraped off.

**So, It's Laughs You Want**

STATESMAN: One who can get into the public's eye without irritating it.

TEA TOTALER: One who adds up your golf score.

TOOTHACHE: The pain that drives you to extraction.

TOMORROW: One of the greatest labor saving devices of today.

YAWN: An honest opinion openly expressed.

WRINKLES: Something other people have, Similar to my character lines.

CIGARETTE; A pinch of tobacco rolled in paper with fire at one end and a fool at the other!

MARRIAGE: It's an agreement wherein a man loses his bachelor degree and a woman gains her master

LECTURE: An art of transmitting Information from the notes of the lecturer to the notes of students without passing through the minds of either

LIEUTENANT COMMANDER: The Lieutenant's wife

CONFERENCE: The confusion of one man multiplied by the number present

COMPROMISE: The art of dividing a cake in such a way that everybody believes he got the biggest piece

TEARS: The hydraulic force by which masculine will power is defeated by feminine water-power!

CONFERENCE ROOM: A place where everybody talks, nobody listens and everybody disagrees later on

ECSTASY: A feeling when you feel you are going to feel a feeling you have never felt before

GROOM: One who spends a lot of money on a suit that nobody notices.

CLASSIC: A book which people praise, but never read

SMILE: A curve that can set a lot of things straight!

OFFICE: A place where you can relax after your strenuous home life

YAWN: The only time when some married men ever get to open their mouth

EXPERIENCE: The name men give to their Mistakes

DIPLOMAT: A person who tells you to go to hell in such a way that you actually look forward to the trip

MISER: A person who lives poor so that he can die RICH!

FATHER: A banker provided by nature

OBSTETRICIAN: stork with a large bill

## Dogs

Those prairie greyhound are fast dogs! They must be, the trees are so far apart!

He's a smart dog. I say, "Are you coming, or aren't you?" And he either comes or he doesn't!

That was the day ole Spot disappeared. He swallowed a bottle of K2R and goodbye, Spot!

He's a fire dog. He locates the hydrants!

He's and aggressive dog. Brought in the dog catcher three-time last week.

I got this dog for my wife. I wish I could make a trade like that every day!

I hear you shot your dog! Was he mad? He wasn't exactly pleased about it!

Hunting dog named Salesman. Changed his name to Sales manager. Now all he does now is sit on his can and bark!

## Doubles

If he says that again, I'll just die.
Now, there you go making promises again.

You keep exaggerating.
Well, I'm only human.
There you go exaggerating again.

We have been partners for a long time
A life time.

Good thing he was home.
Well he wasn't exactly home.
He wasn't exactly home?
Well, you know, he said if I was ever in the neighborhood I should drop in.
So, you dropped in?
Through the upstairs window.

Trust me.
Hey, the last time I trusted you, I got stuck with that fat girl from Cincinnati.
I heard she liked short guys.

I won't be home tonight.
That's the best news I have heard all week.

Hey, leave the girls alone and let's just do our act.
You call this an act?
You don't think I act like this all the time, do you? Just when I'm with you.

I wish I had enough money to buy an elephant.
Now, what would you want with an elephant?
Oh, I don't want the elephant, I just want enough money to buy one.

What makes you so stupid?
I have friends in congress.

Hey, I just came over to meet someone you wouldn't know who that was would you?
No, I just here myself.

I'm just an s smart as the next guy. Can i help it if the next guy is an idiot? That isn't good English, where is your grammar? I think she's home with my grandfather.

**So, It's Laughs You Want**

Are you learning anything?
No, I 'm listening to you.

Did you know everything I breathe, a person dies?
Have you tried a good mouth wash?

SHE: All I want is a man who will look up to me and think I'm attractive.
HE: You don't want a man, you want a near-sighted midget.

One: what happened to your forehead?
Two: I bit myself.
One: on the forehead?
Two: I was standing on a chair.

One: What happened to you head? How did you get the lump?
Two: I told my wife I was going drinking and if she didn't like it she could lump it. She lumped it.

One: I don't want to go out with her. Tell her I'm a bum, I'm no good.
Two: The truth won't help.

Actor: Is there a doctor in the house?
Man, in audience: I'm a doctor.
Actor: How do you like the show, doc?

Actor: Is there a doctor in the house?
Man, in audience: I'm a doctor.
Actor: Ehhh, what's up Doc.?

One: what is he doing?
Two: maybe he was practicing scaring people
One: with that face, he doesn't need any practice.
Can I have a quarter for a sandwich? I don't know, let me see the sandwich

Do you have a dime for a cup of Coffee?
No but I'll manage.

This is the Best hearing aid money can buy. It cost over $500 dollars.
what kind is it?
4:30

Woman: well here I am bright and early,
Man: well you're early any way

**So, It's Laughs You Want**

One: we'll end up in the calaboose.
Two: the what?
One: calaboose, jail, you know steel bars, hard bed, small table, jug of water, stale bread.

What makes you so stupid?
I don't know but it works

One: what are you doing?
Two: I'm clearing my throat I swallowed a bug.

One: If you expect me to do that, you will have to pay me more money
Two: how much am I paying you now?
One: Ten dollars a week
Two: Ok I'll give you thirty dollars a month
One: Ok

One: How do you like that all this time I've been working with an idiot
Two: don't worry you'll get used to it, I Did.

One: what happened to your dust proof, water proof, anti-magnetic, shock proof self-winding watch?
Two: I lost it.

Female: I almost fainted when that guy asked me for a kiss.
Male: well you're going to die when you hear what I have to say.

One: got something to drink?
Two: Water.
One: Water? I'm thirsty, not dirty

She: what are you taking for that cold?
He: make me an offer.

Hey you. are you the lady that sent for me?
No then don't bother me

One: she wanted one of my pictures, so I gave her one.
Two: Which one did you give her?
One: The one of (handsome actor)

One: she has been waiting with open arms.
Two: oh yeah? How late does she stay open?

**So, It's Laughs You Want**

One: How do you like that all this time I've been working with an idiot
Two: don't worry you'll get used to it, I Did.

One: what happened to your dust proof, water proof, anti-magnetic, shock proof self-winding watch?
Two: I lost it.

Female: I almost fainted when that guy asked me for a kiss.
Male: well you're going to die when you hear what I have to say.

One: got something to drink?
Two water.
One: I'm thirsty, not dirty

She: what are you taking for that cold?
He: make me an offer.

Hey, you: are you the lady that sent for me?
No then don't bother me

One: she wanted one of my pictures, so I gave her one.
NO, NO, you stop at 3
I stop at nothing

One: she has been waiting with open arms.
Two: oh yeah? How late does she stay open?

One: Do you know who I am?
Two: No, but wait right here and I'll find out!

You know the people I hate the most?
Who?
People you imitate owls,

## Drunks and Drinking

Honest Judge, I wasn't drunk.
Well, the officer that arrested you said you were trying to climb up a lamp post.
I had to Judge, a couple of alligators were chasing me!

An old drunk stumbles into a confessional. After not hearing anything for a while the Priest knocked on the wall. The drunk said, "Forget it buddy there's no paper in here either."
It was a woman who drove me to drink. One of these days I'm gonna write and thank her.

A drunk was driving the wrong way on a one-way street. A policeman stopped him and asked, "Say, buddy, didn't you see those arrows?" "Honest, Officer," said the man, "I didn't even see the Indians."

A millionaire we all know filled his swimming pool with martini's. He claims you can't drown in it, because the deeper you sink, the higher you get.

Wine, women, and song is too much for me. I'm going to have to quit singing.

I'm going to quit drinking, as soon as I can find a better way to get it down.

But judge, I wasn't drunk. The officer that arrested you said you were trying to climb up a lamp post. I had to, judge, a couple of alligators were chasing me.

The way he's drinking, liquor mortis will set in.

Liquor is slow poison. But I'm in no hurry.

He's dreaming of a tight Christmas.

You may be sober tomorrow, but you'll be crazy (or ugly) for the rest of your life.

Now here is a message for all your beer drinkers around the country. (BURP).

I'm going on the wagon as soon as I find one with a bar.

Whiskey improves with age. The older I get, the better it tastes.

Every time my wife finds a bottle of booze in the house, she throws it in the garbage.... we have the happiest garbage men in town.

He only drinks liquor because he can't find anything else to do with it.

You know how he mixes a stiff drink? He adds starch.

Drunk? He was trying to take his pants off over his head.

What a luscious girl. As a matter of fact, she the biggest lush in town.

This whiskey is aged 8 years and will do the same for you.

**So, It's Laughs You Want**

One: (Pours a large stiff drink)
Two: Who is that one for?
One: I think Willie is going to drop over.
Two: If he drinks that he will drop over.

It's a new group called Te-totalers Anonymous. When you feel, you're going on the wagon, you call them and two drunks will come over and talk to you.

His idea of frozen food is scotch on the rocks.

Don't laugh, he knows what he's doing. Two minutes before the check comes, he'll pass out.

This guy comes home drunk without a cent of his paycheck left. He explains he bout something for the house. "What did you buy for the house that cost $112?" she said. "Eight rounds of drinks," he said.

I never drink before noon. (Look at watch) Fortunately, its noon in Bangkok. I love this watch.

I drink lemonade straight.

One more drink, and she's going to be uncautious.

I'm going to draw my own confusion.

My wife was cleaning and she found a 17-year-old bottle of Scotch. She threw it out, thought it was stale.

This world wouldn't be the same today if the British had gotten drunk the night before they ran up Bunker Hill.

The water is sour.
Don't look at me, I never touch the stuff.

He has a drinking problem. He can't afford to buy as much as he can handle.

Happy New Year!

Happy New Year? It's April!

April? Oh boy, am I in a world of trouble! I haven't been home from the New Year's Party!

Drunk standing under a lamp post "I know you're home Mona. Open the door."

He drank so much scotch he has plaid eyeballs.

A drunk approached the desk clerk at a hotel and said he wanted another room. "Why would

**So, It's Laughs You Want**

What is wrong with the room you are in?" asked the clerk

"It's on fire," said the drunk.

One: Here are your eggs. Would you like some toast with that?
Two: (Holds up glass of scotch) Yes Viva La France

Did you come here to drink or to talk?

Take olive from drink and eat it. Now for an after-dinner drink, (drink)

A jumper cable walks into a bar. The bartender says, "I'll serve you, but don't start anything."

A sandwich walks into a bar. The bartender says, "Sorry we don't serve food in here."

A dyslexic man walks into a bra.

A man walks into a bar with a slab of asphalt under his arm and says: "A beer please, and one for the road."

Two termites walk into a bar. One asks, "Is the bar tender here?"

I don't usually come out here in this condition. I don't usually go anywhere in this condition. But there is a reason for my being intoxicated tonight. I have been drinking all day.

## Dum Jokes

Two antennas meet on a roof, fall in love and get married. The ceremony wasn't much, but the reception was excellent

Two hydrogen atoms walk into a bar. One says, "I've lost my electron." The other says, "Are you sure?" The first replies, "Yes, I'm positive..."

Two cannibals are eating a clown. One says to the other: "Does this taste funny to you?"

Patient: "Doc, I can't stop singing 'The Green, Green Grass of Home.'"
Doctor: "That sounds like Tom Jones Syndrome."
Patient: "Is it common?"
Doctor: "It's Not Unusual."

Two cows standing next to each other in a field. Daisy says to Dolly, "I was artificially inseminated this morning.
"I don't believe you," said Dolly.

**So, It's Laughs You Want**

"It's true, no bull!" exclaimed Daisy.

An invisible man marries an invisible woman. The kids were nothing to look at either.

Deja Moo: The feeling that you've heard this bull before.

A man takes his Rottweiler to the vet and says, "My dog's cross-eyed, is there anything you can do for him?"
"Well," says the vet, "let's have a look at him." So, he picks the dog up and examines his eyes. Finally, he says, "I'm going to have to put him down."
"What? Just because he's cross-eyed?"
"No, because he's really heavy."

Apparently, one in five people in the world are Chinese. And there are five people in my family, so it must be one of them. It's either my mom or my dad or maybe my older brother Calvin or my younger brother Ho-Chin. But I'm pretty sure it's Calvin.

I went to a store to buy some camouflage trousers the other day but I didn't see any.

I went to the butcher's the other day to bet him 50 bucks that he couldn't reach the meat off the top shelf. He said, "No, the steaks are too high."

I went to a seafood disco last week and pulled a muscle.

What do you call a fish with no eyes? A fsh.

Follow your dreams! Except that one where you're naked in class

In just two days from now, Tomorrow, will be yesterday.

Dyslexics Have More Nuf.

Money isn't everything, but it sure keeps the kids in touch

When you work here, you can name your own salary. I named mine, "Fred".

A senior citizen was driving down the freeway, his car phone rang. Answering, he heard his wife's voice urgently warning him, "Herman, I just heard on the news that there's a car going the wrong way on 280 Interstate. Please be careful!" "It's not just one car," said Herman. "It's hundreds of them!"

Also, my short-term memory's not as sharp as it used to be and if that wasn't trouble enough, I think my short-term memory is going bad.

**So, It's Laughs You Want**

A Nation of Sheep Breeds a Government of Wolves!

If walking is good for your health, the postman would be immortal.

A whale swims all day, only eats fish, drinks water, and is fat.

A rabbit runs and hops and only lives 15 years.

A tortoise doesn't run and does nothing, yet it lives for 450 years.

And you tell me to exercise?? I don't think so.

## English Language

**Reasons why the English language is so hard to learn:**
The bandage was wound around the wound.

The farm was used to produce produce. (You may get an error here on your grammar check; it's even confused.)

The dump was so full that it had to refuse more refuse.

We must polish the Polish furniture.

He could lead if he would get the lead out.

The soldier decided to desert his dessert in the desert.

Since there is no time like the present, he thought it was time to present the present.

A bass was painted on the head of the bass drum.

When shot at, the dove dove into the! bushes. (another grammar check)

I did not object to the object.

The insurance was invalid for the invalid.

There was a row among the oarsmen about how to row.

They were too close to the door to close it.

The buck does funny things when the does are present.

A seamstress and a sewer fell down into a sewer line.

To help with planting, the farmer taught his sow to sow.

The wind was too strong to wind the sail.

After a number of injections my jaw got number.

**So, It's Laughs You Want**

Upon seeing the tear in the painting I shed a tear.

I had to subject the subject to a series of tests.

How can I intimate this to my most intimate friend?

There is no egg in eggplant nor ham in hamburger; neither apple nor pine in pineapple.

English muffins weren't invented in England or French fries in France.

Sweetmeats are candies while sweetbreads, which aren't sweet, are meat.

quicksand can work slowly, boxing rings are square and a guinea pig is neither from Guinea nor is it a pig. And why is it that writers write but fingers don't fing, grocers don't groce and hammers don't ham?

If the plural of tooth is teeth, why isn't the plural of booth beeth?

One goose, 2 geese. So, one moose, 2 meese? No. Two moose.

One index, 2 indices?

Doesn't it seem crazy that you can make amends but not one amend.

If you have a bunch of odds and ends and get rid of all but one of them, what do you call it?

If teachers taught, why doesn't preachers praught?

If a vegetarian eats vegetables, what does a humanitarian eat?

Sometimes I think all the English speakers should be committed to an asylum for the verbally insane.

In what language do people recite at a play and play at a recital?

Ship by truck and send cargo by ship?

Have noses that run and feet that smell?

How can a slim chance and a fat chance be the same, while a wise man and a wise guy are opposites?

Your house can burn up as it burns down.

You fill in a form by filling it out

An alarm goes off by going on.

The human race, which, of course, is not a race at all.

When the stars are out, they are visible, but when the lights are out, they are invisible.

Why doesn't "Buick" rhyme with "quick"?

If con is the opposite of pro, is Congress the opposite of progress?
If flying is so safe, why do they call the airport the terminal?

## Entertainers

Before he played the piano, he was hassled by his neighbors. Now he doesn't have any neighbors.

This next comedy team are real wits. Between the two of them they make a halfwit.

Our show received mixed notices. We liked it the audience didn't.

It took us 17 years to build this act. It was a government job.

This next act is really antique, I mean unique. I was right the first time.

The show had a happy ending. Everyone was glad when it was over.

Ventriloquist: We just signed a five-year contract with the (producers of the show or the host of the show).
Dummy: We really hooked them!
Ventriloquist: A five-year contract.
Dummy: It states we will not appear here for another five years.

Announcer: This next act, needs no introduction. He is (take paper out of pocket and read) Subpoena. (Hastily put it away and pull out another read the person's name)

This is a great audience. I wish we had a better act.

We held a dinner in his honor. Actually, it was a fish fry.

## Fat Jokes

He has a reversible jacket. You turn it inside out and it doubles as a badminton court.

He has a lot of pull. He needs it with all that drag

To lose weight, don't put your scale in the bathroom, put it in front of the refrigerator.

I think her dress is suffering from tonsillitis.

I have never seen such a crowd of people in one person in all my life.

He's the only guy I know who can take a shower without getting his feet wet.

Recovering from a terrible accident. She was getting her face lifted and the derrick broke.

She had nine buttons on her nighty, but she could only fasten eight (fascinate)

Drop in again anytime. Just call us first and give us time to get out of the way.

fat lady looking for a seat. Here's two seats down her lady.

The stork delivered him in a U-Haul.

I don't care who you are fatso, get your reindeer off my roof.

I like that rainbow tie. It even has a pot at the end.

Two is company he is a crowd.

He's worth a lot. About $4.00 a pound.
Here he is 200 pounds of silly putty

This guy has more chins than a Chinese phone book.

He was a grade school dropout. The floor caved in on him.

He suffers from an over active fork.

He put on some weight, had to have his shower curtain let out.

His suits are tailor made at Tennessee Tent and Awning.

## Fighting

Boy, did I see a good one at the fights last night! Too bad her husband was with her!

I used to be a fighter. I lost my last fight by decision. I decided I had had enough!

I might be short but I'm shifty!

The best way to stay out of fights is to be the heavy-weight champion of the world!

I climbed into the ring, men howled, women screamed! I forgot to put on my trunks!

Boxing glove cramped my style! How can you pull hair with boxing gloves on!?

Talk about a Sunday punch! When he hits you, you land on your weak end!

First a right cross, then a left cross, then the Red Cross!

Before the fight my manager yelled in my ear, "He beats his wife, his mother, and his kids!" That made me fighting mad! I can't stand to have someone yelling in my ear!

Black eye – Nasty battle with a grapefruit!

You think you're a tough mug, don't you? Well....I mean it must be tough having a mug like yours!

I hit him in the nose and you should have seen him run! He ran? Yeah, but he didn't catch me!

I'm in great shape boss, great shape. Get me a fight with Rocky! I want to fight Rocky! How many time do I have to tell you, you're Rocky!

You always hurt the one you glove!

You know the fight is fixed when your opponent comes into the ring smoking a cigar!

He can't fight. Me and my cousin, two of his friends and three other guys almost beat him

I may not come out alive, but I'm going in there! There's only one thing I want you to do.....talk me out of it!

## Flying

A pilot was suspended for thirty days because he walked up the isle of the plane in front of his passengers reading a book entitled "How to fly in ten easy lessons"

A female flight attendan walked by a male passenger. He slapped her on the rear. She turned and said; "Hey buddy you better watch that!" He said, "I have been for the past forty-five minutes!"

I just flew in from Florida! Boy are my arms tired!

Have you ever stopped to think that this airplane was made by the lowest bidder?

I wasn't concerned until the pilot took up a collection for gas!

I was going to take an earlier flight, but I already saw that movie!

I get dizzy when my barber pumps the chair up too high!

The flight was ok, until I opened the window!

I flew here on a BC 8. I don't know if that is the model or the year it was made!

My nose bleeds when I lick an airmail stamp

The hook of the jet missed the restraining wire as he attempted to land on the carrier. The plane went off the ship and headed for the water. Gradually the plane regained altitude just barely missing a visit to the drink. As the plane pulled up the pilot was heard saying, "ok Lord I'll take over from here"

## Food

We were going to serve chicken for dinner tonight, but it got well.

It's not good for you to eat on my empty stomach.

I had a terrible dream last night! I dreamed I was at a banquet and there were a thousand different kinds of food to eat and I wasn't hungry!

A hot dog is the only animal in the world that feed the hand that bites it!

I was going to make a sponge cake, but I couldn't find a sponge.

Want to join me in a bowl of soup? Only if you get in first!

The best way to make Mexican chili is to pour ice water down his back!

Why don't you join me for dinner....at your house!?

Why don't you come over for dinner...? if you don't mind imposing.

How did you find the steak, sir? Oh, I just moved a few peas and there it was!

Dinner: Waiter, how do you expect me to eat this stuff? Call the manager!
Waiter: It's no use sir, he won't eat it either!

If we had some donuts we could have coffee and donuts! If we had some coffee!

Coffee hot? Should be, it's been cooking since last Thursday!

That meat is fresh. Been fresh for six months!

An apple a day keeps the doctor away. An onion a day keeps everybody away!

That stuff will make you thick to your stomach!

The steaks were the size of manhole covers! And they even tasted like manhole covers!

If the dinner is free and the dinner's not me, tell them I'll be there!

I gained 42 pounds on Neutrasystem. They didn't tell me that box with the food in it was supposed to last thirty days!

## Gambling

Lady Godiva put all she had on a horse.

I don't object to nine aces in a deck. But when he has five and I dealt myself four, well.....

Well, there's plenty more where that money went!

Oh, Aid you! I thought you said FADE you!

He played black jack all night! Didn't get a Black Jack until he goes to the parking lot!

The best get well cards are four aces!

## Golf

I just discovered something that will take ten point off my game!! It's called an eraser!

Have you noticed how carts are taking the place of the caddy? Let's face it, they have three distinct advantages: they don't charge, they don't criticize and they don't count!

Life is a big golf tournament. As soon as you get out of one hole, you head for another.

I play golf, so right away you know two important things about me: I may be a liar, but at least I'm a gentleman.

He's not a golf buff. He's a golf nut!

WHEN YOU HIT GOLF BALL INTO THE AIR: Anybody for a high ball?

Golf. That a good walk spoiled.

The closest I ever came to a hole in one was a six.

I don't need a caddy. I need a compass.

I love playing golf in Alaska. You hit the ball down the fairway and by the time it stops rolling, its 4ft wide!

The hardest thing about golf is getting out of the house to play it.

Does he play a fair game?
Yes, he does if you watch him.

The reason the golf pro tells you to keep your head down is so you can't see him laughing.

## Heckler Stoppers

I hope all your teeth fall out except one – that should stay in for tooth decay.

Didn't I see your tongue hanging in a delicatessen?

It's lucky for you I'm a scholar, a gentleman, and a coward.

How would you like to come out to my car and smell the exhaust pipe?

What a big mouth! He can eat a banana sideways!

He's a mastoid of ceremonies – a pain in the ear.

There are people who are liked wherever they go. He's liked whenever he goes!

A waterproof voice. No one can drown it out!

Short of horsepower and long on exhaust.

Now I know why you're such a successful imbecile. You advertise!

I'd put you in your place, but I don't visit sewers!

I'd break you in half, but I don't want two of you!

Fat man – has a lot of pull. He needs it with all that drag.

How would you like to police up your teeth with a broken arm?

If I had a head like yours and it didn't hurt, I'd sleep it off.

He only uses his head to keep his spine from unraveling.

Take care of him, lady. Men like him don't grow on trees. They swing from them!

After they made him, they threw away the shovel!

Haven't I seen your face on a three-dollar bill?

He's an intellectual giant. And we know how the Giants are doing!

Obnoxious heckler: What's even worse.... he's president of our fan club!

Are those your ears or are you breaking them in for a rabbit?

The next time you were your mouth out – leave it out.

He was born in a gutter and now he's working his way down.

He's the kind of guy who comes into a room, voice first.

**So, It's Laughs You Want**

There's a guy with no brains, flat feet, and no talent. During the war, he was a second Lieutenant.

Thanks son, and you know what kind of son I mean.

I don't know what I'd do without you, but I'd like to try.

He's more trouble than a pigeon with diarrhea!

Don't blame him for shooting off his mouth! He brushes his teeth with gun powder!

He's got a head like yesterday's beer!

Is that you nose or are you eating bananas?

Don't mind him folks! He's nothing but a wolf in cheap clothing!

G'way or I'll surround your head with lumps!

Say, do you remember falling out of a hearse.

BEARDED HECKLER: Why don't you get a shave? You look like an armpit!

Sit down! You make the place look shabby.

How would you like to feel the way he looks!?

Why don't you stick your head out the window – feet first!

Oh, I'm sorry, I didn't recognize you without your leash!

How can you talk all night without stopping to think?

I haven't see you since I quit drinking!

Sir, I know this is an open meeting---but that means guests, not mouths.

Sir, would you mind sitting down? So far, you've had all the impact of a Water Pik on the Chicago Fire.

Sir, has it ever occurred to you that half of communication is listening?

This may be hard to believe, but I happen to know he won the (date two years ago) American Outdoorsman of the Year Award. In (date two years ago), he was thrown out of more doors than any other man in America!

Listen, you, irate buffoon, you couldn't draw a crowd if you were a gutter on New Year's Eve.

## Insults

Yes, I am enjoying myself. There is no one else to enjoy on this show.

Yes, medicine breath

He is the sap in our family tree.

Listen, you, ding dong, I want nothing from you but breathing and very little of that!

What scares me, is that sometimes I catch myself enjoying you.

If beauty were intoxicating, you'd be a whiskey sour.

If brains were intoxicating, you'd be a whiskey sour.

If baloney were snow, you'd be a blizzard.

The last time I saw anything like him, I pinned a tail on it.

He claims he doesn't have any enemies. That may be true, but none of his friends like him.

He is the foul ball in the game of life.

Disliking him is so much pleasure there ought to be an amusement tax on it.

Can I borrow your I.Q.? I'm going to a masquerade party as a moron.

I need you like Custer needed another Indian.

You know, you have that certain. . . nothing!

Say! Aren't you the guy that invented the toothache?

And your crybaby whiny opinion would be...?

Does your train of thought have a caboose?

Whatever kind of look you were going for, you missed.

No matter how thin you slice it, it's still baloney!

## Jokes about jokes

As a child, my mother would stuff my mouth with cotton whenever I cried. There has been a gag there ever since.

He's not a medical student, but he'll keep you in stitches.

He doesn't really steal jokes, he just has a creative memory.

I'm going to give my joke writer a loyalty test.

I've been through more material than Joseph A. Bank.

That's funny. That was my joke during rehearsal.

Hey, I know a good joke when I steal one.

Hey. You wouldn't talk like that if my writers were here.

He was trying out his jokes on me. Sort of a dry run.

The laughed at Thomas Edison, they laughed at Henry Ford. Hey, I wonder who was writing their material?

You see. . . the joke was . . . oh never mind.

That was funny when I thought of it but it didn't sound so funny when I said it out loud.

They sneak up on you folks, you gotta pay attention.

Joke bombs: (take out note pad and pen pretend to write as you say in a low voice): "Note to self. Fire joke writer."

Come on folks, work with me here."

## Law Truisms

**Natural Laws of Frustration:**

**Law of Mechanical Repair:** After your hands become coated with grease, your nose will begin to itch and you'll have to pee.

**Law of Gravity:** Any tool, nut, bolt, screw, when dropped, will roll to the least accessible place in the universe.

**Law of Probability:** The probability of being watched is directly proportional to the stupidity of your act.

**Law of Random Numbers**: If you dial a wrong number, you never get a busy signal; someone always answers.

**Law od Variation:** If you change lines (or traffic lanes), the one you were in will always move faster than the one you are in now.

**Law of the Bath:** When the body is fully immersed in water, the telephone rings.

**Law of Close Encounters:** The probability of meeting someone you know INCREASES dramatically when you are with someone you don't want to be seen with.

**Law of the Result:** When you try to prove to someone that a machine won't work, IT WILL!!!

**Law of Biomechanics:** The severity of the itch is inversely proportional to the reach.

**Law of the Theater & Hockey Arena:** At any event, the people whose seats are furthest from the aisle, always arrive last. They are the ones who will leave their seats several times to go for food, beer, or the toilet and who leave early before the end of the performance or the game is over. The folks in the aisle seats come early, never move once, have long gangly legs or big bellies and stay to the bitter end of the performance. The aisle people also are very surly folk.

**So, It's Laughs You Want**

**The Coffee Law:** As soon as you sit down to a cup of hot coffee, your boss will ask you to do something which will last until the coffee is cold.

**Murphy's Law of Lockers:** If there are only 2 people in a locker room, they will have adjacent lockers.

**Law of Physical Surfaces**: The chances of an open-faced jelly sandwich landing face down on a floor, are directly correlated to the newness and cost of the carpet or rug.

**Law of Logical Argument**: Anything is possible IF you don't know what you are talking about.

**Brown's Law of Physical Appearance:** If the clothes fit, they're ugly.

**Oliver's Law of Public Speaking:** A closed mouth gathers no feet!!!

**Wilson's Law of Commercial Marketing Strategy:** As soon as you find a product that you really like, they will stop making it, OR the store will stop selling it!!

**Doctors' Law:** If you don't feel well, make an appointment to go to the doctor, by the time you get there you'll feel better. But don't make an appointment, and you'll stay sick.

**Law of Light and Sound:** Light travels faster than sound. Therefore, some people appear bright until you hear them speak.

**The Law of fines and taxes:** A fine is a tax for doing wrong. A tax is a fine for doing well.

**The Law of Last laughs**: He who laughs last, thinks slowest.

**The Law of sunshine days:** A day without sunshine is like, well, night.

**The Law of Inevitable Change:** Change is inevitable, except from a vending machine.

**So, It's Laughs You Want**

**The Law of the Sword:** Those who live by the sword get shot by those who don't.

**The Law of the Fool Proof:** Nothing is foolproof to a sufficiently talented fool.

**The 50-50-90 rule:** Anytime you have a 50-50 chance of getting something right, there's a 90% probability you'll get it wrong.

**The Law of California Drivers**: It is said that if you line up all the cars in the world end-to-end, someone from California would be stupid enough to try to pass them.

**The Shoe Law:** If the shoe fits, get another one just like it.

**The Law of those who Wait:** The things that come to those who wait, may be the things left by those who got there first.

**The Law of Fishing Lessons**: Give a man a fish and he will eat for a day. Teach a man to fish and he will sit in a boat all day drinking beer.

**The Law of the Flashlight**: A case for holding dead batteries.

**The Law Finding Furniture in the dark:** God gave you toes as a device for finding furniture in the dark.

**The Law of the Jury**: When you go into court, you are putting yourself in the hands of twelve people, who weren't smart enough to get out of jury duty.

**Life is not the way it's supposed to be - it's the way it is. The way you cope with it is what makes the difference.**

## Lexicon Follies

1. A bicycle can't stand alone. It is two tired.

2. A will is a dead giveaway.

3. Time flies like an arrow. Fruit flies like a rotten apple.

4. A backward poet writes inverse.

5. A chicken crossing the road ... poultry in motion.

6. If a clock is hungry, does it go back four seconds?

7. The guy who fell onto an upholstery machine was fully recovered.

8. You are stuck with your debt if you can't budge it.

9. He broke into song because he couldn't find the key.

10. A calendar's days are numbered.

11. A boiled egg is hard to beat.

12. He had a photographic memory which was never developed.

13. The story of the short fortuneteller who escaped from prison ... a small medium at large.

14. Those who get too big for their britches will be exposed in the end.

15. When you've seen one shopping center you've seen a mall.

16. If you jump off a bridge in Paris, you are in Seine.

17. When she saw her first strands of gray hair, she thought she'd dye.

18. Santa's helpers are subordinate clauses.

19. Acupuncture ... a jab well done.

20. Marathon runners with bad shoes suffer the agony of de feet.

21. The roundest knight at King Arthur's round table was Sir Cumference. He acquired his size from too much pi.

22. I thought I saw an eye doctor on an Alaskan island, but it turned out to be an optical Aleutian.

23. She was only a whisky maker's daughter, but he loved her still.

24. A rubber band pistol was confiscated from algebra class because it was a weapon of math disruption.

25. No matter how much you push the envelope, it will still be stationery.

26. A dog gave birth to puppies in a public place, and was cited for littering.

27. Two silk worms had a race. They ended up in a tie.

28. A hole has been found in the nudist camp wall. The police are looking into it.

29. Atheism is a non-profit organization.

30. I wondered why the baseball kept getting bigger. Then it hit me.

31. A sign on the lawn outside the drug rehab center ... 'Keep off the Grass'

## Love Lines

Do you still love me? Are you still rich? Answer the second question first.

Say you'll marry me and you'll never see me again!

Let's go into the living room and start living.

Don't go away girls, he may be wrong you know.

One: How did you learn to kiss like that?
Two: I used to blow a trumpet.

One: Come up to my apartment and we'll toast the New Year.
Two: The New Year is 5 months away!
One: You don't have to leave early, do you?

One: My eyes said she's beautiful. My heart told me, she's the one.
Two: What do you hear from your liver?

Bye now! Be good and don't make eyes at the delivery man!

Tell me about yourself, your hopes, your dreams, your cellphone number.

Come on up to my room. I want to hate myself in the morning!]

If nobody claims me in 30 days, I'm yours!

Please, you're steaming up my glasses.

Put on some lipstick kid, I need a target.

One kiss from her and you'll never want to waste your lips on eating again!

You think you have pretty lips? Why, I'd put mine up against them anytime!

I always dream of a person like you. What do you eat before going to bed?

We sat on the porch late on evening and watched the moon coming up over her father's long underwear.

Boy: How do you keep a figure like that?
Girl: I never pay any attention to it.
Boy: Boy! You don't know what you're missing!

Boy: Do you want to dance?
Girl: Yes!
Boy: Well, just sit here and maybe someone will ask you.

**So, It's Laughs You Want**

One: Are you going my way?
Two: Yes.
One: Well, you go my way and I'll stay here.

One: Is your friend as cute as you are?
Two: Nobody is!

You look wonderful! This is silly to ask, but, how are you?

You need a defenseless man to protect you!

I couldn't have happened to a nicer girl!

I want to get a present for my wife. If you were a girl, what would you want?

Beautiful girl: Good Morning!
Man: It was good, now its sensational!

I'll meet you in the garden next to the scarecrow. Ah, maybe you better wear a ribbon so I'll recognize you!

I'm not going to fall for just anybody! I'm going to wait for the right girl to come along....and here she is!

Get back here! That was a fast romance!

Man: Am I intruding?
Woman: Yes!
Man: Maybe you ought to wear a girdle!

Woman: Do you dance?
Man: Oh, that's hugging set to music.
Woman: What don't you like about that?
Man: The music.

Man: What's your name?
Woman: Jane.
Man: Can I call you Jane? When?

That was quick! You don't fool, around do you? Do you?

## Marriage

I was married by a judge. I should have asked for a jury.

An un-named woman wrote "Men are like fine wine. They all start out as grapes, and it's our job to stomp on them and keep them in the dark until they mature into something you'd like to have dinner with."

Benjamin Franklin said; "Keep your eyes wide open before marriage, and half shut afterwards."

A man goes to see the Rabbi. "Rabbi, something terrible is happening and I have to talk to you about it."
The Rabbi asked, "What's wrong?"
The man replied, "My wife is going to poison me."
The Rabbi, very surprised by this, asks, "How can that be?"
The man then pleads, "I'm telling you, I'm certain she's going to poison me. What should I do?"
The Rabbi then offers, "Tell you what. Let me talk to her, I'll see what I can find out and I'll let you know."
A week later the Rabbi calls the man and says, "I spoke to your wife on the phone for three hours. You want my advice?
The man said, "Yes" and the Rabbi replied, "Take the poison."

Whatever you may look like, marry a man your own age. As your beauty fades, so will his eyesight.

A bachelor is a guy who never made the same mistake once.

Anyone know what the difference between a boyfriend and a husband is? About 25 pounds.

The difference between a girlfriend and a wife – The smart man would say absolutely nothing!!!!

## Money

It's not hard to meet expenses . . . they're everywhere.

She drives a vehicle that gets $400 to the mile – a 2002 shopping cart!

She thinks like the government – never lets debts keep her from spending more!

She claims she needs a new coat worse than the moon needs a new astronaut!

This is a non-profit organization, but we didn't plan it that way.

The economy is so bad that I got a pre-declined credit card in the mail.

CEO's are now playing miniature golf.

Exxon-Mobile laid off 25 Congressmen.

Angelina Jolie adopted a child from America.

Motel Six won't leave the light on anymore.

A picture is now only worth 200 words.

They renamed Wall Street " Wal-Mart Street"

There's so little money in my bank account, my scenic checks show a ghetto.

Rich? This guy doesn't count his money, he measures it.

What this country needs is a good 5¢ nickel.

Now a days you can get anything with a credit card except money.

Go read your money.

What do you mean a dollar doesn't go far? Have you ever tried getting one back?

Money. That is what you use when you can't find your credit card.

That not his brief case, that's his wallet.

Remember when charity was a virtue instead of an industry?

Well there's plenty more where that went.

I would give a thousand dollars to be a millionaire.

## Old – Growing Old - Senior Citizens

Eventually you will reach a point when you stop lying about your age and start bragging about it.

The older we get, the fewer things seem worth waiting in line for.

Some people try to turn back their odometers. Not me; I want people to know 'why' I look this way. I've traveled a long way, and some of the roads weren't paved.

When you are dissatisfied and would like to go back to youth, Think of Algebra.

You know you are getting old when everything either dries up or leaks.

I don't know how I got over the hill without getting to the top.

One of the many things no one tells you about aging is that it's such a nice change from being young.

One must wait until evening to see how splendid the day has been.

Being young is beautiful, but being old is comfortable.

Long ago, when men cursed and beat the ground with sticks. It was called witchcraft. Today it's called golf.

If you don't learn to laugh at trouble, you won't have anything to laugh at when you're old

Don't worry about old age--it doesn't last that long."

Don't let anyone tell you you're getting old. Squash their toes with your rocker.

Maturity means being emotionally and mentally healthy. It is that time when you know when to say yes and when to say no, and when to say WHOOPPEE!

How old would you be if you didn't know how old you are?

I don't know how I got over the hill without getting to the top.

The golden years are really just metallic years: gold in the tooth, silver in your hair, and lead in the rear.

Life would be infinitely happier if we could only be born at the age of 80 and gradually

approach

One of the many things no one tells you about aging is that it is such a nice change from being young.

Age seldom arrives smoothly or quickly. It is more often a succession of jerks.

Yeah, being young is beautiful, but being old is comfortable.

Old age is when former classmates are so gray and wrinkled and blind that they don't recognize you.

If you don't learn to laugh at trouble, you won't have anything to laugh at when you are old.

First you forget names, then you forget faces. Then you forget to pull your zipper up, then you forget to pull your zipper down.

I realized that at my age I don't really give a rat's rear-end anymore.

Old age is when the liver spots show through your gloves.

You know you're old if they have discontinued your blood type.

These days, I spend a lot of time thinking about the hereafter . . .I go somewhere to get something, and then wonder what I'm "here after".

I'm the life of the party...... even if it lasts until 8 p.m.

I'm very good at opening childproof caps.... with a hammer.

I'm usually interested in going home before I get to where I am going.

I'm awake many hours before my body allows me to get up.

I'm smiling all the time because I can't hear a thing you're saying.

I'm very good at telling stories; over and over and over and over...

**So, It's Laughs You Want**

I'm so cared for -- long term care, eye care, private care, dental care.

I'm not really grouchy I just don't like traffic, waiting in long lines, crowds, lawyers, unruly kids, barking dogs, politicians, and a few other things I can't seem to remember right now.

I'm sure everything I can't find is in a safe secure place, somewhere.

I'm wrinkled, saggy, lumpy, and that's just my left leg.

I'm having trouble remembering simple words like....

I'm beginning to realize that aging is not for wimps.

I'm sure they are making adults much younger these days, and when did they let kids become policemen?

I'm wondering, if you're only as old as you feel, how could I be alive at 150?

You are only as old as you feel like . . . admitting

I'm a walking storeroom of facts.... I've just lost the key to the storeroom door.

I hear my friends saying; "All is not lost." If all is not lost, then where the heck is it?

An elderly couple had dinner at another couple's house, and after eating, the wives left the table and went into the kitchen. The two gentlemen were talking, and one said, 'Last night we went out to a new restaurant and it was really great. I would recommend it very highly.' The other man said, 'What is the name of the restaurant?' The first man thought and thought and finally said, 'What is the name of that flower you give to someone you love? Gardenia? No, the one that's red and has thorns. 'Do you mean a rose? 'Yes, that's the one,' replied the man. He then turned towards the kitchen and yelled, 'Rose, what's the name of that restaurant we went to last night?'

Inside every old person is a young person wondering what happened.

My finest hour lasted a minute and a half.

Old age is coming at a really bad time!

At my age "Getting lucky" means walking into a room and remembering what I came in there for.

**So, It's Laughs You Want**

Funny, I don't remember being absent-minded.

I started out with nothing, and I still have most of it.

My wild oats are mostly enjoyed with prunes and all-bran.

I finally got my head together, and now my body is falling apart.

Funny, I don't remember being absent-minded.

It was a whole lot easier to get older, than to get wiser.

I'm not old I have just been aging for a long time.

Funny, I don't remember being absent-minded.

**Comment from the author:** I don't know where this come from but it is worth publishing here:

**Not Nursing Home for my old Age!**

No nursing home for us. We'll be checking into a Holiday Inn! With the average cost for a nursing home care costing $288.00 per day, there is a better way when we get old and too feeble. I've already checked on reservations at the Holiday Inn. For a combined long term stay discount and senior discount, it's $59.23 per night. Breakfast is included, and some have happy hours in the afternoon. That leaves $228.77 a day for lunch and dinner in any restaurant we want, or room service, laundry, gratuities, and special TV movies. Plus, they provide a spa, swimming pool, a workout room, a lounge, and washer-dryer, etc. Most have free toothpaste and razors, and all have free shampoo and soap. $5 worth of tips a day you'll have the entire staff scrambling to help you. They treat you like a customer, not a patient.

There's a city bus stop out front, and seniors ride free. The handicap bus will also pick you up (if you fake a decent limp). To meet other nice people, call a church bus on Sundays. For a change of scenery, take the airport shuttle bus and eat at one of the nice restaurants there. While you're at the airport, fly somewhere. **Otherwise, the cash keeps building up.**

**So, It's Laughs You Want**

It takes months to get into decent nursing homes. Holiday Inn will take your reservation today. And you're not stuck in one place forever -- you can move from Inn to Inn, or even from city to city.

Want to see Hawaii? They have Holiday Inn there too. TV broken? Light bulbs need changing? Need a mattress replaced? No problem. They fix everything, and apologize for the inconvenience. The Inn has a night security person and daily room service. The maid checks to see if you are ok. If not, they'll call an ambulance . . . or the undertaker. If you fall and break a hip, Medicare will pay for the hip, and Holiday Inn will upgrade you to a suite for the rest of your life. And no worries about visits from family. They will always be glad to find you, and probably check in for a few days mini-vacation. The grand-kids can use the pool. What more could I ask for?

**<u>Old Folks AIDS Warning</u>!**

Senior Citizens are the Nation's leading carriers of AIDS, HEARING AIDS. BAND AIDS, ROLL AIDS, WALKING AIDS, MEDICAL AIDS, GOVERNMENT AIDS, MOST OF ALL, MONETARY AID TO THEIR KIDS!

Not forgetting HIV (Hair is Vanishing)

I don't trip over things, I do random gravity checks!

I don't have gray hair. I have "wisdom highlights." I'm just very wise.

I was complaining about my aches and pains to a friend who is about my age. He said; "Hey at this time in your life, if you wake up and you are not hurting somewhere, go back to bed. Because you're dead!

One of the problems of being my age is telling myself ... "I don't need to write that down, I'll remember it."

Old age is when you choose your cereal for the fiber, not the toy.

My mind not only wanders; sometimes it leaves completely.

## One Liners

Last year I joined a support group for procrastinators. We haven't met yet!

I don't need anger management. I need people to stop ticking me off!

Lord grant me the strength to accept the things I cannot change, the courage to change the things I can and the friends to post my bail when I finally snap!

Never raise your hands to your kids. It leaves your groin unprotected.

I'm always slightly terrified when I exit out of Word and it asks me if I want to save any changes to my ten-page technical report that I swear I did not make any changes to.

I keep some people's phone numbers in my phone just so I know not to answer when they call.

I think the freezer deserves a light as well.

You can lead a horse to water, but remember this . . . remember what a wet horse smells like.

I'm not into working out. My philosophy is no pain, no pain.

I'm in shape. Round is a shape

I wash my clothes in cold water to keep them from shrinking. Now if I could just figure out how to keep my closet from shrinking my clothes I'll be set.

I'm desperately trying to figure out why Kamikaze pilots wore helmets

Do illiterate people get the full effect of alphabet soup?

I've always wanted to be somebody, but I should have been more specific

You have to stay in shape. My mother started walking 5 miles a day when she was 60. She's 97 now and we have no idea where she is

I have six locks on my door, all in a row. When I go out, I lock every other one. I figure no matter how long somebody stands there picking the locks, they are always locking three of them.

**So, It's Laughs You Want**

Commercials show you how detergents take out bloodstains. I think if you've got a T-shirt with bloodstains all over it, maybe your laundry isn't your biggest problem.

Ask people why they have deer heads on their walls and they tell you it's because they are such beautiful animals. I think my wife is beautiful, but I only have photographs of her on the wall.

A lady came up to me on the street, pointed at my suede jacket and said; "Don't you know a cow was murdered for that jacket?" I said "I didn't know there were any witnesses. Now I'll have to kill you too."

I just got skylights put in my place. The people who live above me furious.

Tell a man that there are 400 billion stars and he'll believe you. Tell him a bench has wet paint and he has to touch it.

I went to a bookstore and asked the saleswoman, "Where's the self-help section?" She said, if she told me, it would defeat the purpose.

Raising teenagers is like nailing Jell-O to a tree.

There is always a lot to be thankful for, if you take the time to look. For example, I'm sitting here thinking how nice it is that wrinkles don't hurt.

One reason to smile is that every seven minutes of every day, someone in an aerobics class pulls a hamstring.

Families are like fudge . . . mostly sweet, with a few nuts.

Today's mighty oak is just yesterday's nut that held its ground.

If you can remain calm, you just don't have all the facts.

A day without sunshine is like. . . night.

On the other hand . . . you have different fingers.

I just got lost in thought. It was unfamiliar territory.

42.7 percent of all statistics are made up on the spot.

99 percent of lawyers give the rest a bad name.

**So, It's Laughs You Want**

I Feel I am diagonally parked in a parallel universe.

Honk if you love peace and quiet.

Remember, half the people you know are below average.

Support bacteria. They are the only culture some people have.

Monday is an awful way to spend 1/7 of your week.

A clear conscience is usually a sign of a bad memory.

Change is inevitable, except from vending machines.

Plan a spontaneous tomorrow.

If everything seems to be going well, you have obviously missed something.

When everything is coming your way, you're in the wrong lane.

I hate Indian givers. No I take that back

Eagles may soar, but weasels do not get sucked into jet engines.

I used to have an open mind but my brains kept falling out.

I couldn't repair you brakes so I made your horn louder.

If the world did not suck, we would all fall off.

Aim high, and you won't shoot your foot off.

Tranquilizers work only if you follow the advice on the bottle - keep away from children.

I will accept your apology if you write it on the back of a $20 bill.

Is a frog's ear waterproof?

That's an elephant- ah irrelevant.

**So, It's Laughs You Want**

My wife told me I had to stop acting like a flamingo. So, I had to put my foot down.

What's the difference between a hippo and a Zippo? One is really heavy, and the other is a little lighter.

How do you get two whales in a car? Start in England and drive west.

A blind man walks into a bar. And a table. And a chair.

I bought some shoes from a drug dealer. I don't know what he laced them with, but I've been tripping all day.

Why did the old man fall in the well? Because he couldn't see that well.

I bought the world's worst thesaurus yesterday. Not only is it terrible, it's terrible.

This is my step ladder. I never knew my real ladder.

My friend asked me to help him round up his 37 sheep. I said "40."

I went bobsleighing the other day, killed 250 bobs.

Wife says to her programmer husband, "Go to the store and buy a loaf of bread. If they have eggs, buy a dozen." Husband returns with 12 loaves of bread.

Communism jokes aren't funny unless everyone gets them.

What did the pirate say when he turned 80 years old? "Aye matey."

Have you heard about those new corduroy pillows? They're making headlines.

Two men meet on opposite sides of a river. One shouts to the other "I need you to help me get to the other side!" The other guy replies, "You are on the other side!"

I couldn't figure out why the baseball kept getting larger. Then it hit me.

People in Dubai don't like the Flintstones. But people in Abu Dhabi do!

Guy walks into a bar and orders a fruit punch. Bartender says "Pal, if you want a punch you'll have to stand in line." Guy looks around, but there is no punch line.

I've been told I'm condescending. (That means I talk down to people.)

**So, It's Laughs You Want**

It's hard to explain puns to kleptomaniacs because they always take things literally.

I want to die peacefully in my sleep like my grandfather did, not screaming in terror like the passengers in his car.

Even duct tape can't fix stupid... but it can muffle the sound!

You never really learn to swear until you learn to drive.

No one ever says, "It's only a game", when their team is winning.

Last night I played a blank tape at full blast. The mime next door went nuts.

## One Liner Questions

Why Is it good if a vacuum really sucks?

Why is the third hand on a watch called the second hand?

If a word is misspelled in the dictionary, how would we ever know?

If Webster wrote the first dictionary, where did he find the words?

If something is not out of whack is it in whack?

Why does "slow down" and "slow up" mean the same thing?

Why does "fat chance" and "slim chance" mean the same thing?

Why do "tug" boats push their barges?

Why do we sing "Take me out to the ball game" when we are already there?

Why are they called "stands" when they are made for sitting?

Why is it called "after dark" when it is really "after light"?

Why doesn't "expecting the unexpected" make the unexpected expected?

**So, It's Laughs You Want**

Why are a "wise man" and a "wise guy" opposites?

Why do "overlook" and "oversee" mean opposite things?

Why is "phonics" not spelled the way it sounds?

If work is so terrific, why do they have to pay you to do it?

If all the world is a stage, where is the audience sitting?

If love is blind, why is lingerie so popular?

If you are cross-eyed and have dyslexia, can you read all right?

Why is bra singular and panties plural?

Why do you press harder on the buttons of a remote control when you know the batteries are dead?

Why do we put suits in garment bags and garments in a suitcase?

How come abbreviated is such a long word?

Why do we wash bath towels? Aren't we clean when we use them?

Why doesn't glue stick to the inside of the bottle?

Why do they call it a TV set when you only have one?

Christmas - What other time of year do you sit in front of a dead tree and eat candy out of your socks?

Why do we drive on a parkway and park on a driveway?

How important does a person have to be before they are considered assassinated instead of just murdered?

if a Ham is considered cured What disease did it actually have?

My toaster has a setting that barely warms your bread and the other end burns the toast to a horrible crisp. Why is that when no decent human being would eat it like that?

**So, It's Laughs You Want**

The statistics on sanity is that one out of every four persons is suffering from some sort of mental illness. Think of your three best friends -- if they're okay, then it's you.

Why do I have to press one for English when you're just gonna transfer me to someone I can't understand anyway?

Oops! Did I roll my eyes out loud?

What's the speed of dark?

How come you don't ever hear about gruntled employees?

Why don't they just make mouse-flavored cat food?

What happens when you get scared half to death twice?

Why do psychics have to ask you for your name?

Why do they sterilize needles for lethal injections?

Isn't Disney World a people trap run by a mouse?

Whose cruel idea was it for the word "lisp" to have an "s" in it?

Light travels faster than sound. Is that why some people appear intelligent until you hear them speak?

How come 'abbreviated' is such a long word?

Why do you press harder on a remote-control when you know the battery is dead?

Why are they called apartments (apart-ments), when they're all stuck together?

Why do banks charge you a "non-sufficient funds fee" when they already know you don't have any?

If the universe is everything, and scientists say that the universe is expanding, what is it expanding into?

**So, It's Laughs You Want**

If a tree falls in the forest and no one is around to see it, do the other trees make fun of it?

Why is a carrot more orange than an orange?

Why are there 5 syllables in the word "monosyllabic"?

Why do they call it the Department of Interior when they are in charge of everything outdoors?

Why is it, when a door is open it's ajar, but when a jar is open, it's not adore?

If Superman could stop bullets with his chest, why did he always duck when someone threw a gun at him?

Why does lemon juice contain "artificial ingredients" but dish washing liquid contains "real lemons"?

Why do we wait until a pig is dead to "cure" it?

Why do we put suits in a garment bag and put garments in a suitcase?

Instead of having ballerinas stand on their toes, why don't they just get taller ballerinas?

Do Roman paramedics refer to IV's as "4's"?

What do little birdies see when they get knocked unconscious?

Is boneless chicken considered an invertebrate?

Isn't the best way to save face, to keep the lower part shut?

If you take an Oriental person and spin him around several times, does He become disoriented?

If people from Poland are called Poles, why aren't people from Holland called Holes?

Why do we say something is out of whack? What's a whack?

**So, It's Laughs You Want**

If a pig loses its voice, is it disgruntled?

Why is the man who invests all your money called a broker?

Why do croutons come in airtight packages? It's just stale bread to begin with.

When cheese gets its picture taken, what does it say?

Why is a person who plays the piano called a pianist but a person drives a race car not called a racist?

Why do overlook and oversee mean opposite things?

Why isn't 11 pronounced one-ty one?

If lawyers are disbarred and clergymen defrocked, doesn't it follow that electricians can be delighted, musicians denoted, cowboys deranged, models deposed, tree surgeons debarked, and dry cleaners depressed?

What hair color do they put on the drivers' licenses of bald men?

If it's true that we are here to help others, then what exactly are the others here for?

Ever wonder what the speed of lightning would be if it didn't zigzag?

If a cow laughed, would milk come out her nose?

If olive oil comes from olives, where does baby oil come from?

Why do you have to "put your two cents in". . . but it's only a "penny for your thoughts"? Where's that extra penny going to?

If Jimmy cracks corn and no one cares, why is there a stupid song about him?

Can a hearse carrying a corpse drive in the carpool lane?

**So, It's Laughs You Want**

Why does a round pizza come in a square box?

How is it that we put man on the moon before we figured out it would be a good idea to put wheels on luggage?

Why is it that people say they "slept like a baby" when babies wake up like every two hours?

If a deaf person has to go to court, is it still called a hearing?

Why are you IN a movie, but you're ON TV?

Why do people pay to go up tall buildings and then put money in binoculars to look at things on the ground?

Why do doctors leave the room while you change? They're going to see you naked anyway.

If the professor on Gilligan's Island can make a radio out of a coconut, why can't he fix a hole in a boat?

Why do people point to their wrist when asking for the time, but don't point to their crotch when they ask where the bathroom is?

Why does Goofy stand erect while Pluto remains on all fours? They're both dogs!

If Wyle E. Coyote had enough money to buy all that ACME crap, why didn't he just buy dinner?

If electricity comes from electrons, does morality come from morons?

Do the Alphabet song and Twinkle, Twinkle Little Star have the same tune?
Why did you just try singing the two songs above?

Did you ever notice that when you blow in a dog's face, he gets mad at you, but when you take him for a car ride; he sticks his head out the window?

If the Barbie doll is so popular, why do we have to buy her friends?

**So, It's Laughs You Want**

How much deeper would the ocean e without sponges?

How do you know when you are out of invisible ink?

How many of you believe in psycho-knesis? Raise my hand.

Wouldn't it be great if we could put ourselves in the dryer for ten minutes; come out wrinkle-free and three sizes smaller?

If someone with multiple personalities threatens to kill himself, is it considered a hostage situation?

Is there another word for synonym?

Where do forest rangers go to "get away from it all?"

If a parsley farmer is sued, can they garnish his wages?

Would a fly without wings be called a walk?

If a turtle doesn't have a shell, is he homeless or naked?

Can vegetarians eat animal crackers?

If the police arrest a mime, do they tell him he has the right to remain silent?

How do they get deer to cross the road only at those yellow road signs?

One nice thing about egotists: they don't talk about other people.

Does the Little Mermaid wear an algebra (alge-bra)?

Do infants enjoy infancy as much as adults enjoy adultery?

How is it possible to have a civil war?

**So, It's Laughs You Want**

If one synchronized swimmer drowns, do the rest drown too?

If you ate both pasta and antipasto, would you still be hungry?

If you try to fail, and succeed, which have you done?

Whose cruel idea was it for the word "Lisp" to have "S" in it?

If you spin an oriental man in a circle three times does he become disoriented?

Can an atheist get insurance against acts of God?

Do you ever feel like you are in a dog eat dog world and you're wearing milk bone underwear?

## Paraprosdokian.

Where there's a will, I want to be in it.

Do not argue with an idiot. He will drag you down to his level and beat you with experience.

The last thing I want to do is hurt you. But it's still on my list.

Light travels faster than sound. This is why some people appear bright until you hear them speak.

If I agreed with you, we'd both be wrong.

We never really grow up, we only learn how to act in public.

War does not determine who is right - only who is left.

Knowledge is knowing a tomato is a fruit. Wisdom is not putting it in a fruit salad.

Evening news is where they begin with 'Good Evening,' and then proceed to tell you why it isn't.

To steal ideas from one person is plagiarism. To steal from many is research.

**So, It's Laughs You Want**

A bus station is where a bus stops. A train station is where a train stops. On my desk, I have a work station.

I thought I wanted a career. Turns out I just wanted paychecks.

Whenever I fill out an application, in the part that says, 'In case of emergency, notify:' I put 'DOCTOR.'

I didn't say it was your fault, I said I was blaming you.

Women will never be equal to men until they can walk down the street with a bald head and a beer gut, and still think they are sexy.

Behind every successful man is his woman. Behind the fall of a successful man is usually another woman.

A clear conscience is the sign of a fuzzy memory.

I asked God for a bike, but I know God doesn't work that way. So, I stole a bike and asked for forgiveness.

You do not need a parachute to skydive. You only need a parachute to skydive twice.

Money can't buy happiness, but it sure makes misery easier to live with.

There's a fine line between cuddling and holding someone down so they can't get away.

I used to be indecisive. Now I'm not so sure.

You're never too old to learn something stupid.

To be sure of hitting the target, shoot first and call whatever you hit the target.

Nostalgia isn't what it used to be.

Hospitality is making your guests feel at home even when you wish they were.

I always take life with a grain of salt. Plus, a slice of lemon, and a shot of tequila.

When tempted to fight fire with fire, remember that the Fire Department usually uses water.

## Punography

I tried to catch some fog. I mist.

When chemists die, they barium.

Jokes about German sausage are the wurst.

I know a guy who's addicted to brake fluid. He says he can stop any time.

How does Moses make his tea? Hebrews it.

I stayed up all night to see where the sun went. Then it dawned on me.

This girl said she recognized me from the vegetarian club, but I'd never met herbivore.

I'm reading a book about anti-gravity. I can't put it down.

I did a theatrical performance about puns. It was a play on words.

They told me I had type A blood, but it was a type-O.

I didn't like my beard at first. Then it grew on me.

When you get a bladder infection, urine trouble.

What does a clock do when it's hungry? It goes back four seconds.

I wondered why the baseball was getting bigger. Then it hit me!

Broken pencils are pointless.

What do you call a dinosaur with an extensive vocabulary? A thesaurus.

England has no kidney bank, but it does have a Liverpool.

I used to be a banker, but then I lost interest.

I dropped out of communism class because of lousy Marx.

All the toilets in London police stations have been stolen. Police say they have nothing to go on.

I took the job at a bakery because I kneaded dough.

**So, It's Laughs You Want**

Velcro - what a rip off!

Cartoonist found dead in home. Details are sketchy.

How does Moses make his tea? Hebrews it.

I stayed up all night to see where the sun went. Then it dawned on me.

I'm reading a book about anti-gravity. I just can't put it down.

I did a theatrical performance about puns. It was a play on words.

They told me I had type-A blood, but it was a Type-O.

PMS jokes aren't funny; period.

Why were the Indians here first? They had reservations.

We're going on a class trip to the Coca-Cola factory. I hope there's no pop quiz.

I used to be a banker, but then I lost interest.

Venison for dinner again? Oh deer!

Puns for educated minds:
The fattest knight at King Arthur's round table was Sir Cumference.

I thought I saw an eye doctor on an Alaskan island, but it turned out to be an optical Aleutian.

A rubber band pistol was confiscated from algebra class, because it was a weapon of math disruption.

No matter how much you push the envelope, it'll still be stationery.

My dog gave birth to puppies near the road and was cited for littering.

Two silk worms had a race. They ended up in a tie.

Atheism is a non-prophet organization.

**So, It's Laughs You Want**

A sign on the lawn at a drug rehab center said: 'Keep off the Grass.'

The midget fortune-teller who escaped from prison was a small medium at large.

A vulture boards an airplane, carrying two dead raccoons. The stewardess looks at him and says, 'I'm sorry, sir, only one carrion allowed per passenger.'

## Restaurants

Rice? No thanks, reminds me of one of the saddest moments of my life

Their food is fresh. Yesterday I had to wrestle a lobster for the French-fried potatoes

They have one ingredient in their meat loaf that we don't have. . . Meat!

I used to love their raisin bread, until the other night when three of the raisins flew away.

There is one thing wrong with the eff foo young. It's not egg, it's not young, it is just foo.

The headwaiter picked my table, the waiter picket my food, the door man picked my pocket.

Now isn't that ridicules? Five dollars for a piece of nut cake. If you pay five dollars you belong in the cake.

They use a substitute for margarine.

I used so much artificial sugar, I ended up with artificial diabetes.

They don't add up the bill, they multiply it.

I opened a fortune cookie, and it read "disregard first cookie."

Business was so bad the doorman was arrested for loitering.

Waiter do you serve crabs here?

We serve any one sir, sit down.

We lose money every day, except Saturday. We are closed on Saturday.

We have the only mice in town receiving care packages.

Hey pal, sit down and have a drink. Waiter, bring my pal a glass of water.

Here, they don't call them bouncers, they call them the escort service

## Recession

***Recession is so bad. . .***

I got a pre-declined credit card in the mail.

CEO's are now playing miniature golf.

Exxon-Mobile laid off 25 Congressmen.

I saw a Mormon polygamist with only one wife.

If the bank returns your check marked "Insufficient Funds," you call them and ask if they meant you or them.

McDonald's is selling the 1/4 ouncer.

Angelina Jolie adopted a child from America .

Parents in Beverly Hills fired their nannies and learned their children's names.

My cousin had an exorcism but couldn't afford to pay for it, and they re-possessed her!

A truckload of Americans was caught sneaking into Mexico .

A picture is now only worth 200 words.

When Bill and Hillary travel together, they now have to share a room.

The Treasure Island casino in Las Vegas is now managed by Somali pirates.

Congress says they are looking into this Bernard Madoff scandal. Oh Great! The guy who made $50 Billion disappear is being investigated by the people who made $1.5 Trillion disappear!

## Smoking

I'm a chain smoker myself, can't afford cigarettes.

This cigar is so strong I have to knock the ashes off with a sledge hammer.

He smokes cigars that smell like they are made from old death certificates.

He smokes filter tipped marijuana.

My doctor said ok it's your choice, cigarettes or cancer. Some choice! I gave up cancer!

That's one of those cigarettes with a new filter. Charcoal and sweat socks.

Cigarette smoking is one of the leading cause of statistics.

He decided to smoke only after meals. Of course, he was eating 130 meals a day.

## Sports

One: I'll never forget the time I went big game hunting.

Two: Make that big Dame hunting and I will believe you.

One: No, I went big game hunting the other day. Shot twenty bucks. I should not have drawn on an inside straight.

One: I'll never forget the time I went big game hunting. Oh, yeah, I shot a tiger dead.

Two: How ling had he been dead when you shot him?

One: Hey, watch where you are shooting you almost hit my wife.
Two: Sorry ole man, here take a shot at mine.

The team has a new secret weapon. A ten-foot pole with a white flag on the end.

Talk about team spirit! They lost four games in an ow, but did that deter them? No, they went right back out there and lost four more.

The call him the judge. Spends a lot of time on the bench.

**So, It's Laughs You Want**

Oh this? It's an old football injury. I got drunk during the super bowl game and fell off the couch.

That's the fortune teller I was telling you about. She has three holes I her Chrystal ball. In the evening se used it for bowling.

I wondered how losing ten games in a row did not dampen their spirit. Then someone notice the olives in their water bucket.

We have some players that are good enough to play for us. What we need is some players that are good enough to play for the Chicago Bears.

Do you know why football players pat each other on the fanny? That is the only place where they don't have any broken bones.

I have watched so much football I am wearing out my end zone.

This bad leg? It's an old football injury. I got  drunk the Super bowl game and fell off the couch,

## Wimmin!

***This was a term used by comics in Vaudeville and Burlesque in the late 1800's and early 1900's to express frustration each time they were foiled by a woman in the comedy skit.***

It may be a good thing I don't understand women. Women understand women and they don't like them.

Aren't you too young to be trusted with a figure like that?

She is a high-class lady, the keys to her heart has to fit a Lexus too,

She's a blonde, this week.

It doesn't take much to soften her up, just soak her in money.

Girl with a dog: There goes man's best friend. . . and a dog.

That girl has everything a man could want. . . money.

I have a way with women. No matter how hard they struggle I can always manage to wrap myself around their little finger.

She entered the Miss America contest and lost her citizenship.

Women and cats will do as they please, and men and dogs should relax and get used to the idea.

Wow! That woman is so healthy I get tired just looking at her.

A man goes to a shrink and says, "Doctor, my wife is unfaithful to me. Every evening, she goes to Larry's bar and picks up men. In fact, I'm going crazy. What do you think I should do?" "Relax," says the Doctor, "take a deep breath and calm down. Now, tell me, exactly where is Larry's bar?"

The reason women don't play football is because 11 of them would never wear the same outfit in public.

**9 Words Women Use**

1. Fine: This is the word women use to end an argument when they are right and you need to shut up.

2. Five Minutes: If she is getting dressed, this means a half an hour. Five minutes is only five minutes if you have just been given five more minutes to watch the game before helping around the house.

3. Nothing: This is the calm before the storm. This means something, and you should be on your toes. Arguments that begin with nothing usually end in fine.

4. Go Ahead: This is a dare, not permission. Don't Do It!

5. Loud Sigh: This is actually a word, but is a non-verbal statement often misunderstood by men. A loud sigh means she thinks you are an idiot and wonders why she is wasting her time standing here and arguing with you about nothing. (Refer back to # 3 for the meaning of nothing.)

6. That's Okay: This is one of the most dangerous statements a woman can make to a man. That's okay means she wants to think long and hard before deciding how and when you will pay for your mistake.

7. Thanks: A woman is thanking you, do not question, or faint. Just say you're welcome. (I want to add in a clause here - This is true, unless she says; 'Thanks a lot' - that is PURE sarcasm and she is not thanking you at all. DO NOT say 'you're welcome'. That will bring on a 'whatever').

8. Whatever: Is a woman's way of saying, "Go to Hell".

9. Don't worry about it, I got it: Another dangerous statement, meaning this is something that a woman has told a man to do several times, but is now doing it herself. This will later result in a man asking; 'What's wrong?' For the woman's response refer to # 3.

John was on his deathbed and gasped pitifully, "Give me one last request, dear," he said. "Of course, John," his wife said softly. "Six months after I die," John said, "I want you to marry Bob." "But I thought you hated Bob," she said. With his last breath John said, "I do!"

## Work - Unemployment

Dummy: My brother is in the circus. He gets five hundred a week for swallowing a four-foot sword,

Ventriloquist: What' s So great about that?

Dummy: My brother is only 3 feet tall, then one day he gave it up,

Ventriloquist: He retired?

Dummy: No, he got the hiccups,

Tiera's One big thing wrong with the boss - he's temperamental 90% temper, and 10% mental,

This is a non-profit organization, but it wasn't planned that way,

Dummy: Uncle Charlie Was a circus star, He, the guy they shot out of a cannon,

Ventriloquist: That sounds dangerous, did he get hurt?

Dummy: I don't know, we ain't found him yet!

The Unions are pushing for a 4-day week, who's going to pay for all those coffee breaks I'll be missing.

I have been in the habit. I am getting $500 a meet. Third job rued me at that habit,

I pretend to work. They pretend to pay me. Sarcasm is just one more service we offer.

Errors have been made. Others will be blamed.

A PBS mind in an MTV world.

Well, this day was a total waste of makeup.

Not all men are annoying. Some are dead.

I'm trying to imagine you with a personality.

A cubicle is just a padded cell without a door.

Stress is when you wake up screaming & you realize you haven't fallen asleep yet.

Can I trade this job for what's behind door number 1?

## So, It's Laughs You Want

I thought I wanted a career, turns out I just wanted paychecks.

Too many freaks, not enough circuses.

Macho Law prohibits me from admitting I'm wrong.

Nice perfume. Must you marinate in it?

Chaos, panic, & disorder -- my work here is done.

I plead contemporary insanity.

How do I set a laser printer to stun?

Meandering to a different drummer.

## Yogi Berra Quotes

"It's like deja vu all over again."

"We made too many wrong mistakes."

"You can observe a lot just by watching."

"A nickel ain't worth a dime anymore."

"He hits from both sides of the plate. He's amphibious."

"If the world was perfect, it wouldn't be."

"If you don't know where you're going, you might end up some place else."

"I really didn't say everything I said."

"The future ain't what it used to be."

"I think Little League is wonderful. It keeps the kids out of the house."

"Nobody goes to Ruggeri's, restaurant in St. Louis anymore because it's too crowded."

"I always thought that record would stand until it was broken."

"We have deep depth."

"All pitchers are liars or crybabies."

When giving directions to Joe Garagiola to his New Jersey home, which is accessible by two routes: "When you come to a fork in the road, take it."

**So, It's Laughs You Want**

"Always go to other people's funerals, otherwise they won't come to yours."

"Never answer anonymous letters."

On being the guest of honor at an awards banquet:

"Thank you for making this day necessary."

"The towels were so thick there I could hardly close my suitcase."

"Half the lies they tell about me aren't true."

**O.K. I give up!**

**I hope this helps.**